JOHN BURKE
AND KATHY BURKE

IMAGINE THE GOD OF HEAVEN DEVOTIONAL

60 REFLECTIONS ON THE HEART OF GOD FROM THE BIBLE & NEAR-DEATH EXPERIENCES

TYNDALE
elevate
ask. seek. find.

Visit Tyndale online at tyndale.com.

Imagine the God of Heaven Devotional: 60 Reflections on the Heart of God from the Bible and Near-Death Experiences

Cover design by Dean H. Renninger

Interior design by Brandi Davis

Published in association with Don Gates of the literary agency The Gates Group; www.the-gates-group.com.

For information about special discounts for bulk purchases, please contact Tyndale House Publishers at csresponse@tyndale.com, or call 1-855-277-9400.

Library of Congress Cataloging-in-Publication Data

A catalog record for this book is available from the Library of Congress.

ISBN 978-1-4964-8015-6

Printed in the United States of America

31 30 29 28 27 26 25
7 6 5 4 3 2 1

Introduction

When I (John) first came across near-death experiences (NDEs), I was an agnostic. I did not believe in Jesus, and I thought God probably didn't exist—there was just no evidence. That's when I saw the book that coined the term *near-death experience* on my father's bedside table. He was dying of cancer, and a friend had given him the first book researching when people clinically die, with no heartbeat or brainwaves in many cases, yet they are resuscitated. They come back declaring they were more alive than they've ever felt, in a place more real than earth, and often in the presence of a God of Light and Love whom they never wanted to leave. Many also claimed to meet Jesus on the other side.

I read the book in one night, and it opened my closed, skeptical mind. Because so many in the book talked of God and Jesus, I started to study the Bible, and I eventually came to faith in Christ. Over the past thirty-five plus years, I have studied close to 1,500 near-death experiences, and I went from a career in engineering into ministry, also becoming an intense student of the Bible. In 2015, I wrote the *New York Times* bestseller *Imagine Heaven*, showing how over forty commonalities that people describe during a near-death experience correlate with what God has revealed in Scripture about the exhilarating life to come. In 2023, I wrote *Imagine the God of Heaven* because these people would consistently tell me, "Nothing could compare to being in the presence of God."

The book you hold in your hands is a devotional written by my wife, Kathy, and me based on *Imagine the God of Heaven*. Kathy has been a partner with me in all the books I've written, and she has a spiritual gift of encouragement that will inspire you and build you up. We wrote this devotional to help you meditate daily on the heart and character of God so that you draw closer to God with all your heart. Colossians 3:1-4 tells us, "Set your sights on the realities of heaven, where Christ sits in the place of honor at God's right hand. Think about the things of heaven, not the things of earth. For you died to this life, and your real life is hidden with Christ in God. And when Christ, who is your life, is revealed to the whole world, you will share in all his glory."

That is the aim of this devotional—to help you imagine God as he truly is. We hope these daily reflections help you better imagine God's splendid glory, unconditional love, overwhelming kindness, never-ending patience, extravagant joy, and so many more amazing qualities. We pray you'll realize, "God *is* the love I've always wanted." And you will see just how crazy in love God is with you—his unique child—so that you long to trust and follow him daily because he loves you more than you can imagine and desires the very best for you.

Each devotional reflection focuses on a different aspect of God's heart and character. There is a Scripture verse to anchor the reading and meditate on, as well as short testimonies by people from across the globe who encountered the God of the Bible during their near-death experiences. These testimonies are not meant to replace Scripture, but to add color to what the Word of God already tells us about God's heart and attributes. You will also find an encouraging pastoral reflection to inspire you, along with a suggested prayer—all to help you grow in your relationship with God as you better understand each aspect of his character.

We believe this devotional will help you imagine God more accurately, not because God is imaginary, but because God remains unseen for now. Imagination is God's gift to help us set our minds on what is unseen. We all put God in a box to some extent, and we do that because we are finite and God is infinite; we are time-bound and God is eternal. So our prayer is that this devotional expands your mind and deepens your heart as it helps you "see with faith" what Scripture says about our mysterious, wonderful, extremely loving, and personal God. We hope and pray the words of Scripture come to life as they are illustrated through the eyes of those who experienced what each quality of God felt like in his presence, and we pray our commentary and reflection will inspire you to apply these truths to your life today.

We do not advocate blindly believing what everyone who has had a near-death experience says. In *Imagine the God of Heaven*, I show the difference between what people *report* experiencing and how they may *interpret* what they experience. I have made a strong case in *Imagine the God of Heaven* that the experiences most commonly reported are testimonies to the God of history, revealed through the Jewish prophets and through Jesus. I also make the case in the book for why Scripture should be used to interpret near-death experiences, and not the other way around. However, we hope that the testimonies in this devotional will draw your heart to the reality of God's heart revealed in Scripture, and that it becomes your heart's greatest desire to connect with God's heart.

As you meditate daily on the heart of God through these reflective readings, we pray God's presence would fill and surround you with the love and delight he holds uniquely for you, his beloved child.

Blessings,
John and Kathy Burke

....

May the LORD *bless you and protect you.*
May the LORD *smile on you and be gracious to you.*
May the LORD *show you his favor and give you his peace.*

NUMBERS 6:24-26

1

Boundless Love

May you have the power to understand, as all God's people should, how wide, how long, how high, and how deep his love is. May you experience the love of Christ, though it is too great to understand fully.

EPHESIANS 3:18-19

When people who have a near-death experience find themselves in God's presence, they experience an overwhelming, immeasurable, incomparable love—a powerfully brilliant love, exploding with radiant light, that they struggle to describe with limited human words. Imagine being in the presence of this supernatural love—too amazing for our minds to fully comprehend!

Sarah, a young teenage girl who died in a car accident, experienced God's boundless, extravagant love during her NDE. Prior to the accident, Sarah had suffered abuse during her entire childhood. As the ambulance raced her to the hospital after the crash, Sarah remembers thinking she was going to die and realizing she did not have even one happy memory in her fourteen years of life. Yet during her NDE, she felt the deep and overwhelming love of God. She describes it this way:

> In a flash, the light was coming right at me. . . . I put my hand in first and it felt so incredible. One's mind can't express in words the feelings of immense LOVE. I put the rest of what I sensed to be my body into

> the light, and I was in LOVE! I became ONE with the light. I was held immediately so close and tight. It felt like someone was hugging me. I was thinking I never wanted to leave the light. . . . I allowed my walls to come down for the first time in my life. I allowed myself to get lost in the experience. I danced in the light and spun around. I was so happy to have felt good for the first time in my life. . . . I can't tell you my feelings through all this. I wish I could download it and send it to everyone. Like every particle that is making up who you are is bursting with LOVE and BLISS.[1]

Erica McKenzie describes the same unfailing love of God during her own NDE. After years of battling with an eating disorder and diet pills, Erica's heart started failing one night when she was alone in a hotel room. As a registered nurse, Erica recognized the signs and ran out into the street below, looking for help. A driver pulled over and took Erica to his nearby church where her heart stopped as the pastor called 911. Erica recalls experiencing God's love that night as she never had before.

> I went up and up, and I knew I was going to Heaven. It seemed as if I rose infinitely past the stars and farther into the all-encompassing light until I had finally reached the end of the tunnel. Once there, the most all-encompassing feeling of love overwhelmed me. My human words cannot accurately describe the enormity of the feeling that filled each cell in my body with more love than imaginable. This love was so tangible I could touch it. While I could not see a physical image, I distinguished this brilliant Presence as the voice I had

> heard all my life. . . . It was God. This Presence was so powerful and intense.[2]

Psychiatrist Dr. Ron Smothermon, who was attacked by a man having a psychotic break, remembers the love of God washing over him so powerfully during his NDE. Since that time, he has been filled with a driving passion to share God's love with others.

> All his qualities are contained in his love, *for love is his overarching nature*. And his love is not an enhanced version of human love. . . . It is a love beyond our experience, simply overpowering. . . . It fills you with his essence, and you know him intimately. . . . When your time comes, and it will, it is you and God, and no one else, swimming in an ocean of love. It is hard to describe what happens—you become his love, and you are together in his light. . . . Confronting God's love person-to-person inspires an intense desire to make his love known to every life form in the universe.[3]

....

Scripture says, "God is love" (1 John 4:8). In other words, God is the very definition of what pure and genuine love actually is. Yet it is often hard to fully grasp what this means and how God's supernatural love can revolutionize our lives. Understanding more about God's love and the power it contains is important in experiencing the fullness of life God desires for us.

As humans, we tend to define love based on our own personal experiences of the love we show one another, which we know is fallible and flawed. We must remember that God's love is perfect, and he loves every person with relentless and extravagant love to which no human love can compare!

There is nothing God does or could ever do apart from his love, for love is the essence of who God is. God's love is radiant and brilliant, steady and unchanging, solid and firm, complete and whole. God's love cannot be contained or restrained; when we are filled with it, we are compelled to love others as he does.

Imagine being loved with such boundless love—because you *are*! Today, meditate on how wide, how long, how high, and how deep his love is for you, and allow it to fill every part of you. Right now, God's radiant light of unfailing, never-ending love surrounds you. Feel the warmth of his light and love as you draw near to him today.

PRAYER

Dear God, thank you for loving me with such relentless, perfect love. Help me to feel the reality of your love more and more, as I draw near to you. Please fill every part of me and radiate your love through me to bless others.

2

Our Merciful Forgiver

The LORD, *the* LORD, *a God merciful and gracious, slow to anger, and abounding in steadfast love and faithfulness, keeping steadfast love for thousands, forgiving iniquity and transgression and sin.*

EXODUS 34:6-7, ESV

CEO Randy Kay felt his body shutting down as he lay in a hospital bed with a MRSA (staph) infection and the critical threat of a pulmonary embolism. Randy was a follower of Jesus, yet he was flooded with anxiety about meeting God. Randy knew all his own sins, and the judgment and shame he expected he would experience before God was overwhelming. Yet when Randy's heart stopped for thirty minutes, he cried out the name of Jesus and describes being pulled into God's presence. He felt surprised by the magnitude of grace he experienced as he and Jesus watched a replay of his life.

> In my preconception of God, before Heaven, I thought initially he would judge me, and that he would be disappointed. Because I was seeing in my Life Review . . . the good and the bad, the times I had failed him. And I was looking at the times I had failed, and he told me he had forgiven me, and I looked and said, "Really . . . even that?" He said, "Yes—even that." And I was amazed. . . . Since I've come back, I

> can remember every detail, every facet of Heaven. It was more real than this world. But you know what is interesting? I can't remember when he showed me those failures. I can't remember those times. I asked the Lord, "Why?" He said to my heart, "Because I've removed them as far as the East is from the West . . . gone!" And I realized that he showed me the failures not to condemn me, but to show me the grace of Jesus Christ in all things.[4]

Others who have had a near-death experience report similar incredible encounters with God's grace. Commercial airline pilot Jim Woodford ignored God his whole life, seeking only after wealth and holding little regard for other people. Eventually, Jim contracted Guillain-Barré syndrome, an extremely painful condition that pushed him to his breaking point. One night, he drove out to a field on his horse farm and accidentally overdosed on opioids. Just before his head collapsed on his truck's steering wheel, Jim cried out to God to forgive him, seconds before he died. Jim soon found himself in the presence of Jesus and his guardian angel. The angel was showing Jesus Jim's book of deeds, but only those done out of love for God. Jim realized then he'd prioritized the wrong things, yet he received undeserved mercy and forgiveness, and it changed him.

> Here I am looking at this magnificent being [Jesus]. The angel was holding up the book of my life. I am ashamed to say that with all the resources and wealth that I had and all the kindnesses I could have done, instead I was focused on a life of luxury and accumulation of wealth. . . . I was so full of arrogance. My nickname was "Diamond Jim." I was so

> self-consumed. Overwhelmed with sadness and shame, as I'm crying, the angel said, "James, what did you do with the life God gave you?" I had no answer except remorse and sorrow. Then Jesus turned toward me. And he smiled at me. He *smiled* at me . . . and when I looked into those eyes of gray, green, blue—I saw such sadness for the way I had lived my life—such sadness for the way mankind has disregarded our Father's message. But I also saw love for me. Forgiveness. And in his eyes, I saw my tomorrow . . . and I was forgiven. . . . I've been given the rarest of second chances, and this time I'm doing it right. From that moment forward, whatever happened, I was his.[5]

....

No matter what we've done or will do, we are never too far gone from God's forgiving reach. He will always forgive us and give us a reset whenever we turn back to him. God honors a humble and willing heart that admits wrong and desires to change. In fact, he not only forgives us, but he gives us a completely fresh start, never holding our wrongs against us.

This is such a radical departure from our human ways. We hold grudges, keep lists of wrongs, often desire revenge, and might even find pleasure in forcing penance on someone who has hurt us. But this is not God's way—God is a forgiver. "God made you alive with Christ, for he forgave all our sins. He canceled the record of the charges against us and took it away by nailing it to the cross" (Colossians 2:13-14).

Jesus paid for all our wrongs, so that "now there is no condemnation for those who belong to Christ Jesus" (Romans 8:1). He forgives, offers restoration instead of condemnation, and removes the wrong. Surrendered to him, we can become all he created us to be. He still allows us to experience the consequences of our mistakes so we can learn from them, but he walks through them with us, guiding us as we are restored to his perfect will for our lives.

We don't need to fear admitting our wrongs to God—he already knows everything about us. He loves us completely, and nothing we could do would ever change that. However, our unconfessed sin saddens him, because it keeps us from experiencing his will and ways in our lives. But as 1 John 1:9 says, "If we confess our sins to him, he can be depended on to forgive us and to cleanse us from every wrong" (TLB).

God is never overwhelmed by your failures, and he will always welcome you back into his loving guidance as you seek his presence in your life. God says, "I will never fail you. I will never abandon you" (Hebrews 13:5). So today, trust him with your failures and ask for his help to overcome. He loves you and will welcome you with open arms—no questions asked, no grudges, no condemnation. Remember, you may be overwhelmed by your failures, but God is not. He forgives them all through Christ, so that you will turn back to him.

PRAYER

Dear heavenly Father, thank you for your love and forgiveness offered to me every moment of every day. I confess my sins to you, and I want your leadership over my life. Thank you for guiding me in your loving will and ways to be the person you created me to be.

3

A Heart God

When a prayer or plea is made by anyone among your people . . . then hear from heaven, your dwelling place. Forgive, and deal with everyone according to all they do, since you know their hearts (for you alone know the human heart).

2 CHRONICLES 6:29-30, NIV

Pilot Jim Woodford grew up in a Catholic family in Newfoundland, but he never prayed. Jim admits, "My one goal in life was to have things. I had a yacht, an airplane, and nineteen British sports cars that I kept in the garage on my horse farm. I enjoyed things, but never once did I even have an urge to talk to God." All this changed when Jim accidentally overdosed and died. With his last breath, he cried out to God, and his experience in heaven with his guardian angel forever changed his perspective about the importance of prayer.

> I looked up in the sky, and it was a cerulean blue—it was a sunless sky, deep, deep blue, and I spotted something like streaks of brilliant light going straight up. [To me] as a pilot, they looked like the white contrails of ice left behind by jets. I thought, *Are those contrails?* I was stunned, seeing six contrails across the sky. I asked the Guardian [angel], "What are those?" And he said, "James, those are the prayers of your family for your soul, as we speak." When I got back, I found

> out my family all came to the house and six of them prayed, "If it be the will of Jesus, please send Jim back." And I was in Heaven seeing those prayers. . . .
>
> We came upon a beautiful building made of the same shimmering material as the others. I asked the angel, "What is this magnificent building?" He replied, "James, this is the hall of knowledge. It is the repository of all the prayers and petitions that mankind sends to Heaven and the throne of God." I was reassured again that nothing is ever lost to God.
>
> So the knowledge spoken of is God's knowledge of the heart of man and his deepest longings, which are cataloged there. Along with prayers, there were accounts of the deeds of people both good and evil. Again, nothing is lost to God. The halls of knowledge are where the books of each of our lives are kept.[6]

Dean Braxton, a youth probation supervisor, became septic during a routine kidney stone procedure that led to an hour and forty-five minutes of clinical death. He shares that during his NDE, he was traveling very fast on his way to heaven, and just like Jim, he saw prayers from his loved ones like shooting stars. Dean went before the throne of God, where he witnessed something profound: Our prayers reach into God himself, because prayers from the heart matter to God.

> The prayers of people who were praying for me were moving faster than I was. . . . They were like shooting stars passing me. . . . The prayers went straight to the throne and the Father. Not only did they go to Father God, but they went inside him. To try to understand this, you will have to realize that the throne of God is

> not a seat. It is a place. He is the throne! There were millions upon millions of prayers entering the Father. I saw these lights of prayers like shooting stars entering the Father. I came to understand that he answers our prayers with himself.
>
> Jesus downloaded information into me about prayers. I saw mighty warring angels, and I knew that prayer is what moved them. God hears our prayers and sets angels into motion in response.* I understood that our prayers must come from our hearts. Our God is a heart God, and he is looking for us to talk to him from our hearts. He hears us if we are praying from our hearts. He hears your heart. He understands your heart. He only hears prayers from the heart.[7]

....

God is a heart God. Jesus reminds us of this in his remarks about the Pharisees: "These people honor me with their lips, but their hearts are far from me" (Mark 7:6). These religious leaders prayed flowery, eloquent prayers for people to hear and admire, but their prayers were not from the heart at all, and God knew it.

God wants our hearts, poured out to him in prayer—honest and humble communication is what God desires from his children. And the encouraging news is that every prayer from the heart matters to God! No genuine, sincere prayer spoken is ever lost to God, for it goes into the very heart of the Father. He promises, "If my people who are called by my name will humble themselves and pray and seek my face and turn from their wicked ways, I will hear from heaven" (2 Chronicles 7:14). Our

---

* In Daniel 10:12 an angel was sent because Daniel prayed.

humble, heartfelt prayers set things into motion in the unseen realms. And the Father responds, sending his angels into action, moving heaven and earth to accomplish what is best for us and others for whom we pray.

It is comforting to know that we don't have to "get it right" to move the heart of God. We don't need to say the right combination of words, or be convincing or eloquent—we just have to be ourselves and be sincere as we communicate to our loving heavenly Father. We don't always see the direct answers to our prayers, but we must not let that stop us. God is recording every prayer so that one day in heaven, we'll be able to see that God did answer every one. Yet he did it in a way that respected the free will and choices of all those involved, working it for the good of us, others, and the world.

Take some time today to pray from your heart. Don't worry about your words—God will understand you perfectly no matter how you express yourself. As you pray, feel his heart filling yours with his love in response, and hear his heart give you heavenly wisdom. Remember, he is always ready to encourage, guide, and support you as you draw near to his heart through prayer.

PRAYER

Father in heaven, you alone know my heart. Thank you that I can bring all that's in my heart to you, and you will hear me and draw near. Here's what's on my heart today, Lord, and help me hear what's on your heart too.

4

Healer of the Soul

He heals the brokenhearted and bandages their wounds.

PSALM 147:3

Kevin Zadai had an unexpected reaction to anesthesia during dental surgery and suddenly found himself above his body, having a near-death experience. While Kevin observed his own surgery, Jesus appeared and began talking with him about darkness in his soul that had been caused by lies spoken over him as a child. Jesus saw the deepest parts of Kevin and offered him healing.

> [Jesus said], "Kevin, there's a part of you called your soul that is hindering you." And he showed me my spirit. My spirit was lit up [with light], and I had this robe of righteousness on me, but I also saw this black part of me, and he said, "Kevin, do you see how that's obscuring your beauty?" And I said, "Yes." He said, "That's your soul. Look real closely."
>
> And when I looked really closely, I saw all these words, these phrases and statements that were spoken. And I remember them being spoken to me when I was a little child. People said things, and they actually cursed me, and they said things that weren't true about

> me. And they changed the way that I perceived God, and my whole observation of this life was tainted by the enemy, because people had spoken wrong [untrue] words over me. People would say things like, "You're never going to amount to anything."[8]

While Kevin was unconscious for forty-five minutes, Jesus showed him how things in his mind needed to be renewed for his soul to be healed.

> [Jesus] said, "We've got to take care of this. . . . You need to build yourself up, praying in the Holy Spirit and staying in the love of God. And then you need to always meditate on the Word of God, and you need to allow your mind to be changed."[9]

When Kevin came back, he began meditating on God's Word as Jesus told him to do, and he has experienced deep healing and a restored identity.

Dr. Colin Perry had grown up a Christian but turned away from God as a young adult, smoking marijuana and occasionally doing hard drugs. Eventually, he left that lifestyle behind, got married, and even got his PhD. But he also experienced a great deal of hardship. His first wife left him, and then three years later, his seven-year-old daughter was struck by a car and left brain-damaged, unable to walk or talk.

While gardening one day, Colin felt his heart failing. As he died, Colin remembers calling out for help and being pulled upward into the presence of Jesus.

> And I looked back to Jesus because I couldn't take my eyes or attention off him. I wanted to know more, and

> he said to me, "I need to do some work, some healing, on you. You've been through a lot of trauma." He then started to . . . I don't know how to explain this . . . it was like Jesus' whole being just came into me and began to shift things around, break down barriers, rearrange things within me. And I could feel, literally feel, things within my soul restoring and healing. It was a beautiful and amazing sensation.[10]

....

God is a healer, and Jesus demonstrated this by miraculously healing people while on earth. In life, we often seek physical healing if something is physically wrong. But there's a healing of the soul Jesus wants to do in us that may be even more important.

Internalized words, curses, lies, and traumas left unhealed can hinder God's work in and through us, keeping us from experiencing the fullness of joy God wants us to have. God will shine his healing light into the hearts of his children who long for healing. Just as Jesus asked the man paralyzed for thirty-eight years, "Do you *want* to get well?" (John 5:6, NIV, emphasis added), he asks us the same. We must be willing to let him search out and rearrange the deepest recesses of our souls. In the presence of his light of love, the wounded, infected parts of our souls *can* be made whole.

It is also comforting to know that no matter what physical or mental challenges our earthly lives may continue to hold, one day in heaven, we will experience the complete healing we have longed for all our lives! Where do you need healing in your soul today? Sometimes facing what needs healing feels scarier than staying wounded. Have you asked the Healer to show you what needs his touch, and are you seeking his healing? Today, share your longings with God, and allow the Healer to restore you to wholeness in him.

PRAYER

Dear God, thank you that you heal my broken heart and gently bandage my wounds. Show me areas of my soul that need healing, and help me to trust you. Thank you that you will restore my wounded soul and make me whole again.

5

Sovereign over All

I am God, and there is none like me. I make known the end from the beginning, from ancient times, what is still to come. I say, "My purpose will stand, and I will do all that I please." . . . What I have planned, that I will do.

ISAIAH 46:9-11, NIV

Dr. Mark McDonough was only a teenager when he had his near-death experience. After trying to rescue his mom and younger brother from a house fire, Mark fell to the ground unconscious with burns over 65 percent of his body. Later, while undergoing surgery at the hospital, his heart stopped, and he left his pain-racked body.

> I felt the presence of God—a love that is just so difficult to put into words, but a sense of love and security that's almost indescribable. Everything is okay. It always has been, it is now, and it always will be, and there's nothing to be afraid of.[11] It had seemed like time stopped. Now I didn't want time to start. . . . I just wanted to linger in this blissful state. . . . All things—past, present, and yet to be—had a specific purpose and reason. . . . Everything was perfect, exactly as it was intended from the beginning of time and would remain so forever. And all of this was so plainly apparent that I felt like giggling at the

simplicity and impeccability. *Oh . . . God! Of course! Who else?*[12] . . . The euphoria, the happiness, the laughter—as quickly as I could think of a question, the answer was there. And the answers were so simple, so joyful, and so clear. I thought, *Oh, yes, of course—that makes complete sense. It all fits together and makes perfect sense. And I'm right where I should be, and things are just the way they should be. It's going to all work; it's all going to be okay.*[13] . . . And I knew that God was saying, "This is a difficult challenge, but it's one we can do together, and I'm with you. I won't leave you." [With] the provision of the Father, and my buddy, Jesus, we're going to make this. It's not going to be easy, but we're going to do it together.[14]

God sent Mark back into what would be a very challenging life ahead. He would be a teenager with no mother, suffering through excruciatingly severe burns that would require over thirty surgeries to repair. Yet despite these hardships, Mark had this assurance: God would work everything out for good, and he was not alone in his suffering. God was with him.

Diana Shepherd had a massive panic attack that stopped her heart in the gym at USC. Jesus sent her back from her NDE, and later during a time of prayer, Diana felt Jesus give her an analogy about God's sovereignty and our choices:

When we choose Jesus, we also have choices to make within his plan. He works with us; however, he guides it overall. Like a mobile navigation app. The navigation app would be like the Holy Spirit you've decided to download. Jesus decides on locations but gives you routing options. The routing options all end

> in the same place, but there are different things you'll see along the way—different obstacles, different paths, all leading to the destination. You make the choice of which route. Think of all the choices we make throughout the day. Jesus knows of alternate routes and plans for them all, depending on your choice. Now multiply that by billions of people. That is a snapshot of just how incredible and smart, brilliant, really, our God is![15]

....

God is sovereign. He's not bound by time like we are, and his knowledge and power are so great that he can accomplish all he purposes for the ultimate good of everyone, even while taking into account the billions of decisions and choices we all make each day. Knowing the loving heart and character of God can bring great peace and confidence—even in the chaos and sufferings of life—reminding us that we are safe with him.

God is always with us, even when we don't acknowledge his presence in our lives, and he will oversee our lives in line with his plan. He's promised that he "causes everything to work together for the good of those who love God and are called according to his purpose for them" (Romans 8:28). As we love and follow God, we can be confident that he will accomplish every good thing he has promised, and one day in his presence, we will understand how the trials and difficulties of our lives worked together for our good and the good of humanity.

Let this truth give you assurance that you can and will accomplish everything that God has planned for you, as you follow his guidance to the best of your ability each day. And if you happen to make a mistake and wander off God's path, just admit it and turn back to him for forgiveness and guidance as soon as you realize it. Similar to how GPS can reroute you to your destination, God's Holy Spirit has an infinite number of ways to get you back on track! Today, allow the powerful sovereignty of God to bring you comfort and confidence as you walk out his plan for your life with him as your guide.

PRAYER

Lord, sometimes I worry that my bad decisions or even my difficulties have ruined your plan for my life. Thank you for your promise that you can make good out of every situation and will get me back on your path as soon as I turn back to you. Help me follow your leadership today and rest in the peace and comfort that your guidance brings.

6

The Light of Glory

The city has no need of sun or moon, for the glory of God illuminates the city, and the Lamb is its light.

REVELATION 21:23

Psychiatrist and neurologist Dr. Ron Smothermon had just returned home after a week-long lecture series in Bristol, England. His friend Amin had been house-sitting for the week. Little did Ron know, Amin had suffered a psychotic break, and he attacked Ron when he walked in the door, stabbing him multiple times. During Ron's near-death experience, as he felt time stop, Ron describes experiencing the explosive light of God's glorious presence:

> I notice over [Amin's] left shoulder a hallway appeared. It is made of something that appears to be solid light. Strangely, I am calm and not attached to the outcome of this insane event. *That looks like infinity,* I thought, as I neared death. The light explodes into being, blocking my view of Amin and the hallway—brighter than the sun, yet not hurting my eyes. It is not an ordinary light; it is a living being, a *who*, not a *what*.
>
> If this person of light came down that hallway, he must have traveled at warp speed. The light itself is a

> person, exactly my height. Instantly, the qualities of this person are written across my awareness. . . . I am stamped with the knowledge of the nature of God. I do not have to wonder about the identity of this light. There is no room for doubt. This is God.[16]

Ron goes on to describe the infinite love, knowledge, power, authority, humor, kindness, joy, purity, and humility of God that were instantly imprinted on his soul. Ron says, "Wrap these qualities in his light, and you have the glory of God."

Ron is not alone. In fact, many people who have had near-death experiences say the glory of God shines brighter than the most brilliant sun and radiates from everything in heaven, infusing every created thing. Ron describes it this way:

> God is truly glorious, magnificent, awesome, without equal. His glory is a light but made of infinite love. God's light appears like a sudden, silent, atomic bomb blast of white light, full of his power. Imagine being five feet away from the source of a nuclear explosion. But his light is more than light—it is overwhelming, a literal tsunami of infinite, unconditional love. All it touches transforms into perfect peace, and [it] blows away into irrelevancy any consideration about what is happening, replacing it with ineffable ecstasy, irresistible joy, love beyond comprehension—all in a singular package. A nuclear bomb blows life away. God's love blows death away.[17]

....

The glory of God shines brighter than the most brilliant sun and is inseparable from his magnificent, unconditional love and the awe-inspiring life that flows from him. People like Ron who have had NDEs say the light, life, and love of God radiate from everything in heaven. Imagine experiencing this exuberant glory of God when you are in his presence!

Even more, believers will not only stand in awe and reverence before his glory but will also *share* in his glory. Romans 5:2 says, "Because of our faith, Christ has brought us into this place of undeserved privilege where we now stand, and we confidently and joyfully look forward to sharing God's glory." What a day that will be!

Perhaps the closer we grow in our relationship with God on earth, and the more we allow his light and love to shine through us now, the greater capacity we are developing to share in his glory in heaven. It is inspiring to think about! After all, Jesus promised that "the righteous will shine like the sun in their Father's Kingdom" (Matthew 13:43).

Today, take a moment to meditate on the mystery and majesty of God's glory, and imagine God's love, life, and light filling every fiber of your being. As you focus on this, make a commitment to do your best to glorify God in all your thoughts and actions, radiating his love and light to all around you. And remember, as a believer you will share in his glory forever!

PRAYER

Dear God, I am in awe of your radiant, glorious presence and humbled by your love for me. Help me to praise you in all I do and say, and let my life shine the light of your glory on all those who cross my path.

7

Full of Delight

Take delight in the LORD,
and he will give you your heart's desires.

PSALM 37:4

When Jim Woodford found himself in heaven, he was overwhelmed with beauty and a sense of home. He shares, "I think God does everything he can to delight us, and he realizes it is such a tremendous event for us to be in his paradise."[18] Jim and others who have had near-death experiences describe heaven as a city surrounded by beautiful countryside. "I remember it, and it becomes so vivid it overwhelms me," Jim recalls.[19] While Jim's body lay slumped over the steering wheel of his truck after an accidental overdose, Jim's spirit was escorted by three angels, one of whom Jim calls the Guardian. The Guardian had been assigned to Jim at conception, and he knew Jim intimately.

> The Guardian invited me to walk with them. They turned, and a beautiful path ten to twelve feet wide opened up, with magnificent flowers on both sides and colors we have no description for. And as we are walking along, they showed me the flowers and I commented on how beautiful the scent was. . . . I then noticed what I thought was music coming from

the flowers. I could hear this tinkling, like gentle bells, but it had a melody. I asked, "Is that music I hear?" He looked at me with those violet eyes and said, "Yes, James. The flowers of Heaven are so happy you're here; they're singing to you."[20]

God knows each soul intimately, so he tailors our experience to the life we had on earth. . . . So for me, [the angel] asked me to touch his cloak and we rise up. . . . It was so beautiful, they gave me an aerial view of Heaven, I suppose because I was a pilot, and I [enjoyed] holding patterns over cities.[21] . . . I'm looking down on the Holy City, and yes, the streets are paved with gold, but it's a different gold. . . . It's a gold with all impurities removed, just as all impurities are removed from our souls. It was translucent, like a golden glass. Stunningly beautiful.[22]

We came back down and resumed the walking, and we came to a split-rail fence like you'd see on any farm. Again, God tailors the experience to your earthly life, and I've always loved horses. The Guardian said, "James, look!" and from behind a group of trees came three of the most magnificent horses I'd ever seen. They trotted up to the gate, and the grass lit up as they ran across.[23] . . . I think why he showed me the horses is because I grew up with them. I've loved them all my life and they've been a big part of my life.

[Then] the angel hugged me . . . and his wing pulled me in. . . . Being hugged by an angel of God is like being hugged by fifty grandmothers at once, and while he hugged me, I smelled tapioca. . . . God is so gentle with us. He remembered when I was a little boy in Newfoundland, . . . I'd go to my grandmother's home and there would be a big warm bowl of tapioca for me.[24]

. . . .

God delights in his children and loves bringing them joy! It may feel challenging to see the goodness of God because there is so much happening in the world that opposes his ways, but everything about God desires the best for us. He wants us to enjoy all the good gifts he gives us and maintain a posture of gratitude toward him—the one who created us to share in his joy.

Sometimes, we might fear that if we follow God with all our hearts and delight in him first, we will miss out on something. As near-death testimonies like Jim's remind us, we will not miss out on anything when we follow God! He delights in giving good things to his children, just like we delight in giving gifts and joyful experiences to our kids—their first birthday cake, gifts on Christmas morning, riding a bike, chasing bubbles, or a special adventure together. God delights in us enjoying his blessings too. As we enjoy the good experiences God gives us and express gratitude, it brings a huge smile to the face of God.

Today, take some time to appreciate all the things you love, and thank God for blessing you with these gifts and passions. These blessings could be your cozy home, your loyal best friend, your talent, or activities you enjoy, like cooking, working out at the gym, or a special hobby. There are endless possibilities! Your heavenly Father gave these gifts and interests to you for a reason. Practice gratitude today for the delights he has chosen especially for you to enjoy.

PRAYER

Thank you, Father, for all the ways you delight in me and for personally giving me blessings and experiences that you know will bring joy to my heart. Guide me to enjoy my life with you, the giver of all good things.

8

Our Marvelous Creator

You made all the delicate, inner parts of my body and knit me together in my mother's womb. Thank you for making me so wonderfully complex! Your workmanship is marvelous—how well I know it. You watched me as I was being formed in utter seclusion, as I was woven together in the dark of the womb. You saw me before I was born. Every day of my life was recorded in your book. Every moment was laid out before a single day had passed.

PSALM 139:13-16

Heidi Barr grew up in a secular Jewish household with an abusive father. He was also a respected lawyer and atheist who tried to pass on his unbelief and mockery of Jesus Christ to his three daughters. It didn't work. From as young as she can remember, Heidi prayed to God every night, and she felt like God comforted her.

When Heidi was sixteen, she rode her horse, Heather, on a hillside trail. Charged by another horse, Heather flipped over backward, crushing Heidi. Although her sisters watched in horror as she died, Heidi found herself fully alive and in the presence of the God she had always known was there.

> I noticed a light over my right shoulder. This light was a golden light, bathing everything before me in a golden hue, lighting up the entire scene. . . . I turned to look, and I saw a man floating there with me, up

in the air. I stared at his face. He smiled. I smiled. He moved forward until he floated right by my side.

I recognized him immediately. How could I not? This was the man, God, who had been at my bedside every single night. . . . I remember saying to him, "Hi! I know you!" There was no doubt in my mind, not one. This man was, without question, Jesus, or Yeshua. His was the name I'd never been allowed to utter in my home, at least not in a way that acknowledged him as anything other than a hoax. My heart overflowed with happiness at our reunion. What a joyous occasion! He grinned at me, every bit as happy as I was, happier, because he is all joy, and he is all happiness. . . .

How we laughed together! We were thrilled to be reunited. I was once again the child I'd been when he would wrap me up in his light, soft as a cloud, and rock me to sleep. I felt exactly the same—safe and surrounded by his loving Presence. Jesus was all at once my Father, my brother, my best friend. I had known him my entire life. He was everything to me.

In that eternal moment, I didn't think of the bad things that had happened; they didn't matter in his Presence. My mind and my heart and my soul were focused on him and on how much he loved me. He loved me for no reason. . . . I hadn't prayed to Jesus. Ever. And I'd turned my back on God in my teenage hurt and confusion. . . . Yet, here he was! Just loving me.

Jesus offered me a life review—except, rather than the story of my life progressing from start to finish in chronological order, I saw my life all at once, from the moment of conception to the present day. He had been right beside me. . . .

> It was during my life review that I saw him by my side, from the moment of my conception. He formed me in my mother's womb. I saw him there. "For it was you who formed my inward parts; you knit me together in my mother's womb" (Psalm 139:13, NRSVUE). I didn't read that psalm until a few years after I'd died.[25]

....

As Heidi discovered, there is only one Creator, and he has revealed himself through Jesus. "The Son is the radiance of God's glory and the exact representation of his being, sustaining all things" (Hebrews 1:3, NIV). As Paul says, "For in him we live and move and have our being" (Acts 17:28, NIV). He is the life force sustaining your life, and through the highs and lows of life, he has always been there with you. No one "gets you" more than the one who made you. Penny Wittbrodt felt this during her NDE. Jesus told her, "You can't take Me out any more than you can take out your own father's DNA. I made you. I'm in there."[26]

When you create something, you're proud of it—you treasure it because it originated from you. This is true if you create a song, a work of art, an idea, or a business—and especially if you conceive a child. God is *your* Creator. God created you as his unique masterpiece—a one-of-a-kind work of art (Ephesians 2:10). He formed you and shaped your soul, and you have intrinsic value given by your Creator that no one in the world can take away.

Even though our broken, sinful world may have caused you harm and even damage, God still sees his perfect masterpiece in you! You are a precious work of art, waiting to be fully restored to the beauty and splendor he had in mind before you were conceived. Do you believe him? Starting this moment, surrender to Jesus, and let him restore you to the beautiful masterpiece he created you to be.

PRAYER

God, thank you for creating me as your valuable, priceless work of art. Help me to see the masterpiece you saw in me when you formed me in my mother's womb, and help me believe you, not the world around me, about my worth to the Maker of my soul. I submit myself to you, so that you can restore in me all that you created me to be.

9

The Savior of the World

We have seen and testify that the Father has sent his Son to be the Savior of the world.

1 JOHN 4:14, NIV

Swidiq Kanana grew up in Rwanda, Africa, as the son of a Muslim sheik. He became an Imam in his twenties, a leader in the mosque, and a gifted apologist for Islam. All this changed, however, when he had a mental breakdown. Swidiq's mother took him to a witchdoctor, but when nothing worked, in desperation she asked the Anglican church to pray to Jesus, for him to save her son. Swidiq was soon cured and became curious about Jesus.

Several months later, Swidiq experienced severe pain in his abdomen and was taken to the hospital. While there, he clinically died from an aggressive blood cancer.

Swidiq shares what happened next:

> On the evening of February 27, about 8 p.m., I became terribly alert. A horrible sensation like nothing I had known was washing over me. . . . And then I went. I was gone from my body. Dying itself was not nearly so bad as the process leading up to it. It was very . . . seamless. . . .

> As I turned my head, I saw [a man with] sandaled feet and a white robe. . . . I was captivated by him, totally uninterested in anything else but the sight of this person. The one now standing in the room, wearing a long white robe, looked just like the Jesus of *The Passion of the Christ*, the film by Mel Gibson. I had once gotten a deal for three American films dubbed in Kinyarwanda, and the first one in the lineup had been *The Passion*. Although I was a Muslim and had no interest in seeing the Jesus story, I had gone ahead to get my full money's worth.
>
> And now he stood there, looking at me. His face was serious and intent on me—the kind of expression that holds absolute authority—but the flicker of a smile or perhaps delight played across all his features. He stood a moment just looking at me. Whether it was just an instant or a long time, I don't really know. . . . At some point, he lifted his hands slightly, with palms up, revealing holes in each hand. Then he raised his right hand and gestured towards me. With lifted hand at last he spoke, clear and firm, "I died for man. And you are among those I died for. Do not deny it again. You must tell others. Reveal it." . . . Then he disappeared.

Swidiq returned to his body. He pulled a sheet off his face, climbed off a table, and then realized he was wearing nothing but a loin cloth. He had been dead for over twelve hours, and a large gathering of Muslims was about to lay him in the grave.

> I began shouting, "Jesus is here! Jesus is here! . . . He brought me back! It was Jesus who got me and

> brought me back!" That was too much for this crowd of terrified Muslims. They began running hysterically in all directions.[27]

After this dramatic resuscitation, Swidiq's heart was forever changed. He went on to become a follower of Jesus and is an Anglican pastor in Rwanda today, enduring persecution and constant danger as an ex-Muslim leader.

....

All people are created by God, and he desires for all to come to know him personally. "For this is how God loved the world: He gave his one and only Son, so that everyone who believes in him will not perish but have eternal life. God sent his Son into the world not to judge the world, but to save the world through him" (John 3:16-17). God loves everyone equally, no matter their religious background, ethnicity, or geographical birthplace.

If you've never made the decision to follow Jesus, acknowledge that you want what Jesus did on the cross to count for you, too. Tell him in your heart right now. And if you already follow him, take some time today to humbly reflect on the grace and mercy bestowed on you through Jesus, your Savior. Thank him, and strive to never take his gift of salvation for granted. He loves you so much that he died for you as if you were the only one.

In gratitude for salvation freely given to you, like Swidiq, let this compel you to want to share his saving, loving grace with all who don't know him yet. As David expressed in Psalm 70:4, "May those who love your salvation repeatedly shout, 'God is great!'"

PRAYER

Dear Lord and Savior, thank you for dying on the cross for my sins and for the sins of the whole world. Help me to share this good news with all who don't know you yet, so they can live forgiven and free in your grace and mercy too.

10

God's Deeply Personal Love

O LORD, you have examined my heart and know everything about me. You know when I sit down or stand up. You know my thoughts even when I'm far away. You see me when I travel and when I rest at home. You know everything I do. You know what I am going to say even before I say it, LORD. You go before me and follow me. You place your hand of blessing on my head. Such knowledge is too wonderful for me, too great for me to understand!

PSALM 139:1-6

While Dean Braxton was clinically dead for an hour and forty-five minutes due to sepsis, he found himself in God's presence and had an extraordinary experience about how God views us personally and loves us uniquely, as if each of us is the only person on the planet.

> I saw the love he has for me, like it would go on and on and on. . . . The moment he looked at me he loved me, and the next moment he loved me more. . . . What got me was he only loved me. . . . I knew he loved the others, but it seemed like he only loved me. . . . And I started thinking about others. I thought about my wife . . . and I saw the love he had for her like he only loved her. . . . Anybody I thought of in the

switch of my thinking, I saw the love he had for them like he only loved them.

Somebody will say, "Did you see the nail prints?" I saw them, but that's not what I was concentrating on. What I was concentrating on was the love coming out of every part of him for me, like I was the only one he loved.[28]

When I finally looked at him, his eyes met my eyes. I remember looking into his eyes, thinking, *He loves me so much, by the time I'm thinking of him loving me, it's old news because he even loves me more!* I used to think he just loves you, and that was it, but it's a growing love every moment, uniquely for you.[29]

I came to understand the day that we are formed within our mother, that God Almighty goes out and creates love for us that only we can receive—it's individually tailor made. And that's what I was receiving, that love that God had tailor made for me.[30]

That light coming off him—I remember it wrapping itself around me. Someone asked me one time was he hugging you, and I said, "Everything about him was hugging me."[31] You know he has cared for you forever and will care for you forever.[32]

Commercial airline pilot Jim Woodford also experienced this overwhelming personal love from Jesus, when he clinically died from an accidental opioid overdose and found himself in Jesus' presence.

For a split second, when he smiled at me and I realized he loved me, and I loved him, my intellect knew better, but it felt like I was the only one that he had

ever created. There was that instant connection. . . .
You are his child.[33]

Deborah Weiler didn't know God before she died, yet she encountered a deeply loving, personal being in her NDE. She shared, "That being knew all of everything I ever was and loved me. Not just loved me but everything that defined me as myself, unique from any other bit of creation, was wonderful to [him]."[34] Deborah was sent back, but she now realized the great worth she had to this compassionate best friend. Years later, her husband encouraged her to read the Bible, where she discovered her friend's identity: Jesus.

....

God created us all special and unique, and we are wonderful and beautiful in his sight. He desires to have a personal relationship with every person he created, even those who have yet to come to know him. His love for us is personal and infinite, as though each of us were the only one he created. When you've felt pure love—genuine, self-sacrificing love, for another person or from another person—this love actually came from God. As the apostle John wrote, "We love each other because [God] loved us first" (1 John 4:19).

It may seem hard to fathom that God, our Creator, loves each and every one of us this much, but he truly does. God's love is extremely personal. Jesus said he even knows the number of hairs on your head (see Matthew 10:30). He knows when you sit and when you stand, when you lie down and wake up (see Psalm 139:2). He longs to share a two-way personal relationship with you, where you feel close enough to share your deepest desires as well as the simple, daily joys of life. He loves experiencing life together with you!

Today, talk to him like you're talking to your loving, devoted Father who is crazy about you, his wonderful child. Allow yourself to experience the limitless love he has in his heart to give uniquely to you. The psalmist wrote, "How precious are your thoughts about me, O God. They cannot be numbered! I can't even count them; they outnumber the grains of sand!" (Psalm 139:17-18). God loves to think about you; you are his beloved. He longs to spend time with you; you are his treasure. As you think about God loving you in such a personal way, let it compel you to love him back.

PRAYER

Thank you, God, that you love me in such a personal way. I am unique and precious in your eyes, and you call me your child. Help me to bring you into my daily life and deepest desires, receiving your encouragement, blessing, and love for the unique things in me you created.

11

Overcomer

Thanks be to God! He gives us the victory through our Lord Jesus Christ.

1 CORINTHIANS 15:57, NIV

Randy Kay suffered greatly as a child. He was constantly in the hospital for severe asthma. He was overweight and bullied. Then when his friend Jimmy was put in the hospital by these same bullies, Jimmy's family moved away and Randy lost his only friend. Years later when Randy was an adult, a pulmonary embolism crashed his heart and he was dead for thirty minutes. During Randy's near-death experience, Jesus reviewed these painful scenes with Randy. Randy recalls how true it is that Jesus overcomes all of earth's suffering.

> "Why? Why did that happen, Lord? It was like a living hell to me then."
>
> "I see not only what is, but what is to come. I knew that the boy who was bullied, [Randy], would grow into the man who would be tenderhearted to the broken of this world. Was it worth it, My beloved?"
>
> "Yes, Lord. It was more than worth it, as I see it now. I had forgotten that painful time in my life until You showed it to me here. I don't remember any of the

> painful things that happened. But I'm glad that You are showing them to me because I see how You turned my wasteland into paradise and even purpose. Thank You for not abandoning me, Lord, even when I had abandoned You."
>
> "Beloved, I knew your heart. I always turn that which is bad for good, for those who turn to Me, even if it takes a lifetime." . . .
>
> "Lord, his [Jimmy's] family went to church. They seemed like model Christians, but You allowed my best friend to be attacked for a reason?"
>
> "Beloved, I redeemed it. Evil reigns only for a season. . . . I will turn good from evil for those who know Me. Beloved, I knew yours and Jimmy's futures, because I could see into your hearts and your hearts determined who you would become."
>
> I didn't need an explanation from Jesus as to why bad things happened under his watch. I knew without any doubt that in the scheme of eternity, even the worst sufferings are nothing in Heaven. I also knew that the blessings of turning evil to good, far outweigh the pain of the world, for all who place their trust in God.[35]

Kevin Zadai had a near-death experience caused by an allergic reaction to anesthesia during dental surgery. He came back with this reminder from Jesus:

> He showed me all the things that are happening against people down here. I said, "Lord, you know, it's hard down there." He said, "Yeah, but it's not about you, Kevin. It's about the people that I'm sending you to. If you tell people what you saw, it's going to help

> them and reroute their lives." He said, "I am going to send you back, and I want you to tell your story, and [I] want you to start to reroute people's lives so that they finish right." . . . Jesus wanted to show me how we can walk in the Spirit, we can walk in love, and finish right. . . . Jesus told me, "The Father and I love everyone. We aren't doing any of these terrible things that are happening to people on the earth. That's the devil doing that. Go back and tell people that it's the god of this world doing all these things."[36]

Dr. Mark McDonough clinically died after trying unsuccessfully to save his mother and brother from a house fire that burned 65 percent of his body. In God's presence, Mark said it all made sense. But when Mark returned, he went through tremendous suffering as a teenage burn victim with PTSD, no mom, and endless reconstructive surgeries to overcome. All this led Mark to grow up to become a plastic surgeon, able to help heal and minister to burn victims with unique empathy. Here is how Mark experienced the suffering in God's presence and how he sums up his perspective on everything he's been through:

> Everything was perfect, exactly as it was intended from the beginning of time and would remain so forever. . . . It was wonderful to be free from pain, but even that which I'd experienced did not matter anymore. And it was hard to even categorize it as bad. . . . *No suffering is ever in vain. All pain has its purpose and is part of the plan.*[37]
>
> God wants us to know we can do anything with His help. He will help us through anything, but He

> doesn't just dump stuff on us so we can prove how strong we are. He does that so we can be sculpted and molded and forged into the being and character He'd like us to be. . . . I want people to realize the joys far outweigh the pain, and it's worth it.[38]

....

It is comforting to know that all the devastation, confusion, and troubles of this life will ultimately be redeemed and restored through God's perfect plan. Remember, God has already won the victory over every evil, so the troubles around us are only temporary!

Jesus promised us that in this world, there will be trials and troubles, but they won't last forever. As Romans 8 explains, our broken world labors under the birth pains of disease, disorder, and the dark forces of evil—for a time. Sometimes we may misinterpret what's happening to us and think God is "doing it to us." Yet even though God seems to allow things that we don't understand, he does so only for a time and for a purpose, and we *will* understand someday. Today we can be confident that he is working in all ways and in all things to bring about the victory that he has already won.

When Jesus died and rose from the dead, he overcame sin, death, and every trial and hardship we would ever face. Through him, we can become overcomers too. As we trust in him, God will turn all of it into something good; he will redeem and restore all that has been lost. We can trust him in the process as we persevere, knowing we can overcome anything with him and through him.

That's why Paul could say, "We can rejoice, too, when we run into problems and trials, for we know that they help us develop endurance. And endurance develops strength of character, and character strengthens our confident hope of salvation. And this hope will not lead to disappointment. For we know how dearly God loves us" (Romans 5:3-5). God, the Overcomer, has made you an overcomer too! Today, if you are going through difficult times, trust him, hold onto these truths, and follow your Overcomer through to victory on the other side.

PRAYER

Lord Jesus, thank you for the promise that in you, I, too, will overcome. As I face the challenges and even sufferings ahead, help me trust your promise that you are working it all for good. Help me hold tightly to you, even when I'm tempted to give up, and know that one day I will see the victory you have already won for me.

12

Prince of Peace

I have told you all this so that you may have peace in me.
Here on earth you will have many trials and sorrows.
But take heart, because I have overcome the world.

JOHN 16:33

College professor Dr. Colin Perry had a near-death experience when his heart failed while he was gardening. He found himself in the presence of Jesus, who exuded deep wisdom, love, and unfathomable peace. Yet, when Jesus asked Colin if he wanted to continue on to heaven or go back to earth, Colin felt fear and anxiety creep back into his thoughts. As his earthly worries returned, the angels' reactions shocked him.

> The response was really quite amazing. The angels all came towards me and started to calm me. And they said, "We're not used to that emotion [fear/anxiety] here. . . . It's out of place here, so please, be calm, be still, and don't be afraid. And they were talking me out of my fear into a state of peace and joy, which for them is the norm. I could hear their thoughts directly in my thoughts, so it was a very direct link. I could feel the fear subside. I could feel that beautiful sense of peace and joy welling up inside me, and I knew that Jesus and the angels were the source of that celebratory

> feeling—that I'm so happy to be here. That was the norm for them.[39]

Catherine was diagnosed with a massive bilateral pulmonary embolism and deep vein thrombosis. After a week in the hospital, her body shut down, and she had an NDE. In Jesus' presence, the word *peace* took on a greater meaning.

> I sensed that I was in another dimension and experienced peace that surpasses all earthly understanding. It is a peace that we don't have or understand here on earth. We call it "peace" because it is the only word we have to describe that deep sense of "peace" that I felt. I saw a soft, bright light shining deep from my spirit. It was like a white light that was shining onto me from above. Another light was next to me on my right-hand side. Somebody was standing there in the shape and form of a human being, but the person was a white light and from the same origin as the White Light I saw in my spirit. I felt as if a Life Force was drawing me to him. I knew it was God. Then he was standing next to me. Immanuel God was with me, and I felt whole and complete in him. It was like a homecoming.[40]

....

Jesus is the Prince of Peace. The Jewish prophet Isaiah foretold his coming: "He will be called: Wonderful Counselor, Mighty God, Everlasting Father, Prince of Peace. His government and its peace will never end" (Isaiah 9:6-7). Peace as we know it on earth is usually the temporary reprieve from fear, strife, anxiety, or fighting, but the peace that comes from God is supernatural and eternal.

God's peace is a soul-settling assurance that all is complete and whole, nothing is lacking, and everything is resolved. In God's peace, there's no need to fight because everything is right and nothing is wrong. In God's peace, all those unsettled feelings of not fitting in, not being accepted, or not belonging have no place, because we are home—where we belong. We can trust that God is in control and that we are safe with him, so there's nothing to fear or worry about. And we can feel that peace now.

Jesus told us his heavenly peace is available to us even here on earth. He promised that even though on earth we will have troubles, *in him* we can have a peace that overcomes. How do we tap into this peace from above? Paul tells us, "Don't worry about anything; instead, pray about everything. Tell God what you need, and thank him for all he has done. Then you will experience God's peace, which exceeds anything we can understand. His peace will guard your hearts and minds as you live in Christ Jesus" (Philippians 4:6-7).

Take a moment today to reflect on the areas in your life where you need God's peace. You may be struggling with worries, fears, or anxieties that are displacing the peace God wants to give you. In gratitude, surrender those to him. Remember, he has already conquered them through Jesus, and he already sees the victory that lies ahead for you! You can stand firmly on his promise that in Christ, you are already safe and secure because the Prince of Peace rules your heart. In this moment, allow his peace to wash over you, guarding your heart and mind with his presence.

PRAYER

Jesus, the Prince of Peace, thank you so much for overcoming this world and all its troubles. I acknowledge and thank you for all the ways you've taken me through life's trials in the past, and I give you my worries, fears, and anxieties of today. I receive your peace as I draw near to you.

13

A Heart of Kindness

The LORD is righteous in everything he does;
he is filled with kindness.

PSALM 145:17

Many people who have had near-death experiences come back sharing about a life review they experienced in the presence of God. Although the details differ, they all return describing a love that supported them through it and the surprising lack of judgment they felt from God. However, they clearly see their right and wrong, and the impact their actions had, whether for good or for evil. And they *all* experience how much little acts of kindness matter to God.

Erica McKenzie collapsed from heart failure in a church office. She shares that as the pastor prayed for her, she left her body and found herself in the presence of God. Once Erica had been filled up to the brim with God's overwhelming love, God gave her a life review as she wore "God-glasses," which allowed her to see her life from the perspective of what matters most to God.

> I saw myself helping an elderly person with their groceries, comforting a friend in need, saying something kind when others were mean, standing up

> for the unwanted, advocating for those who couldn't find their voice, and being a patient listener to those who desperately needed to be heard. It was giving the homeless money when I didn't have money to give and putting others, often complete strangers, first over my own needs because my heart told me it was the right thing to do. It was having a huge heart for all animals, giving love to them, rescuing, and caring for them in times of need. . . . I felt the immediate effect of my words, thoughts, and actions on others. A great majority of these things I did not remember I had done because they were mostly things I did when no one was looking. But God was looking. I understood in that moment that these things were displays of love, kindness, and compassion. They were the only things that mattered in God's eyes. They all required love. Love was the answer to everything![41]

Gregg Rickert, a successful high-end home builder, was hit head-on one night while driving home. After being taken to the hospital, he was put into a medically induced coma. While in the coma, Gregg says he left his body and floated up through what looked like exquisite custom-made entryway doors into heaven, where he learned valuable lessons from Jesus about what's truly important to God.

> I see two people in front of me. One is Jesus and the other is my guardian angel. . . . A three-foot book opened under the portal, and I started to see my book of life displayed in the portal. We were reviewing the things written down in my life's book. He showed me good things and bad things. I realized I had been

> striving for the wrong things—earthly perfection, the nicest house, the coolest car, or the most beautiful wife. None of it has any meaning once you're in Heaven.
>
> I felt welcoming, caring, loving feelings from him. I was in the absolute understanding of my life and experienced how important little things truly are. What really matters. You're being judged in that moment by being allowed to see the importance of what we do and how we live, and how our choices matter. It's very humbling to see life so clearly.[42]

....

Kindness matters to God because it is a direct reflection of his love. The infinite loving-kindness of God toward all his creation overflows without measure, for he is the source of all kindness and goodness. Dr. Ron Smothermon, who had an NDE during a brutal attack, said, "You probably know someone who is kind. If you can, magnify that kindness one thousand times, that's God's kindness."[43] The apostle Paul shares about the power of God's kindness as he says, "His kindness is intended to turn you from your sin" (Romans 2:4).

When we show kindness to any of God's creatures, we reflect the pure and loving nature of God's heart. And kindness can take many forms—from generosity and empathy to consideration and concern for the well-being of others. Every act of kindness is noticed by God, especially acts of kindness toward those who seem to deserve it the least. "If you are kind only to your friends, how are you different from anyone else?" Jesus asks (Matthew 5:47). We can strive to mirror the kindness of God, who generously bestows love and compassion even upon those who are undeserving.

Sometimes you may feel like your selfless actions and kindnesses go unnoticed, especially if you are in a role that requires constant care for others. But remember, no matter what your situation or daily routine looks like, all you do in service to God matters eternally and has lasting impact in the world! The purposeful time spent with your children, the birthday card you bring to an office colleague, the meals you prepare, the laundry you wash and fold, the lunches you pack, the encouraging text message you send, the meal for a sick friend, and even a smile for an unfriendly neighbor—all these, big or small, count in God's eyes.

And Jesus says we are actually interacting with God himself in these times: "When you did it to one of the least of these my brothers and sisters, you were doing it to me!" (Matthew 25:40). Therefore, *every* act of kindness matters, and even the smallest actions done in love are never wasted in God's world.

Today, focus on the truth that every act of kindness toward others is an act of kindness toward God. And every thoughtful act, no matter how small, is a direct reflection of God's heart. This is a simple yet profound way to reflect who God is to the world! So today, let your acts of kindness be acts of worship to God and radiate his love to those around you. You will find that your heart will be filled with his kindness, and others will be blessed with his presence.

PRAYER

Dear God, I realize how important it is for my actions and choices to reflect your kindness to humanity. Thank you for noticing the small things I do for others as big things in your eyes. Help me to always choose kindness and serve others in a positive way, knowing this is directly loving you in the process.

14

God's Love Song

For the LORD *your God is living among you. He is a mighty savior. He will take delight in you with gladness. With his love, he will calm all your fears. He will rejoice over you with joyful songs.*

ZEPHANIAH 3:17

During Dean Braxton's near-death experience, he witnessed the most amazing, surprising serenade at the throne of Almighty God.

> I was there when we all gathered around the throne of God to tell our Father how much we love him, . . . and we got to individually tell him in Song how much we love him. . . . This wasn't in my belief system, I didn't know it was in the Bible at the time, but he sang a love song back to us—each and every one of us. . . . The Song of Solomon in the Bible where two lovers are singing back and forth to each other—that's what it was like. As I was telling him how much I loved him, he was telling me how much he loved me.
>
> It was so personal. Literally, I felt like Heaven was made *just* for me. When you get there, you're going to feel like it was made just for you.[44]

Bill Smith, a musician who uses his passion for music to glorify God, describes a similar experience at the throne of God during his NDE.

> He brought me to a place of peacefulness where it was just me and him. His love for me was just about him and me at that point. . . . I became part of his love. He serenaded me and sang me to his throne. I saw that he was my Song, and Lord God and Savior.[45]

....

The Bible is the greatest love story ever told. And just like we express our devotion to another with love songs here on earth, God does the same and sings love songs to his beloved—us.

The Old Testament prophet Zephaniah says that God delights in us, loves us, and rejoices over us with songs (Zephaniah 3:17). Isaiah 62:5 says, "As a bridegroom rejoices over his bride, so will your God rejoice over you" (NIV). God likens himself to a groom who is so excited to finally be with his bride that he cannot help himself—he bursts out in song! Imagine God loving you this much—longing to be with you and even singing about his love for you.

Over the centuries, the church fathers and commentators have pondered the meaning of the book Song of Songs in the Bible, reaching diverse opinions on its intention and interpretation. The Song of Songs is widely thought to be an extended love poem or love song celebrating Solomon and his bride and the intimacy of marital love. But many biblical scholars claim that it is also a metaphor of God's heart of intimacy for his beloved—all believers—or those he calls his "bride."

Each of our earthly loves, whether it is the nurturing, caring, understanding love of a parent or friend, or the loving passion of a spouse, cannot compare to God's unique love for every one of us. God is crazy in love with you, and he has a special love song just for you and you alone. Maybe this isn't easy to think about if you have never experienced this kind of personal love before. But today, try to imagine the love song God is singing just for you. He loves you so personally and has created love just for you, because he wants you to feel how cherished and special you are to him.

PRAYER

Dear God, thank you for loving me so much that you sing love songs you've written just for me. I want to receive them and sing love songs back to you in gratitude. Your love is greater than anything else I could long for.

15

Awesome in Power

You are the God of great wonders!
You demonstrate your awesome power among the nations.

PSALM 77:14

God is the omnipotent, all-powerful Creator of everything—past, present, and future. Dr. Ron Smothermon encountered the immensity of God's power during his near-death experience. He describes God's power like standing five feet from the source of a nuclear explosion. Ron realized the only fitting response to such a powerful presence was complete awe and reverence.

> In an instant out of time, I see the qualities of the LIGHT, His qualities. However, the experience of these qualities is not something I can give you, for their essence cannot be rendered in words. . . . Imagine trying to describe the Grand Canyon, the Milky Way galaxy, or an atomic bomb blast to a blind person. . . . GOD's LIGHT appeared like a sudden silent fusion atomic bomb blast, pure white and full of His POWER.
>
> His qualities project themselves with perfect clarity and you are better able to receive Him than

> eyes can detail vision or ears define hearing. . . . With His LOVE came certainty of INFINITE POWER. If encountered without INFINITE LOVE, His INFINITE POWER would provoke pure terror; you would surely "fear" GOD. . . . The response His POWER calls forth is Surrender.
>
> In the smallest space of time, perhaps outside time, I knew: This is the One who created universes of unfathomable dimensions, the One who created reality, time, you, and me. . . . He has the moral right to use His POWER, for it comes wrapped in His INFINITE LOVE. . . . The Scriptures tell us to fear GOD. When you meet Him person to person, fear transforms into respect. If you cannot respect GOD, you do not know Him, and then you had best fear Him.[46]

....

The power of God is an awe-inspiring reminder of *who* this infinitely kind, loving Being truly is. He is deserving of the utmost honor, respect, awe, and even fear. And it's not that we *should* or *ought* to feel awe and respect, but that we *will* on the day we stand before God face-to-face. And properly imagining God in all his power helps us to cultivate a deeper, more loving awe and respect for God today.

It is good to reflect on the greatness of God and how he is able to do all things no matter the circumstances. God's overarching power has no comparison, yet his supreme power is used only in love. This is hard to imagine since human power is rarely guided by love. But know that your Creator, the Almighty God, is not only omnipotent and sustaining all things, but he is also present with you always and desires to walk with you and personally guide you through the ups and downs of life. Remember, you are his beloved child.

Today, meditate on how our all-powerful, mighty God is also our loving Father. He loves and cares for you, knows you perfectly, and is able to do anything and everything necessary for your ultimate well-being. Nothing is impossible for him! Jesus himself said, "Humanly speaking, it is impossible. But with God everything is possible" (Matthew 19:26).

This truth can give you great assurance and confidence when life feels out of control, or when fear and worry find their way into your heart and mind. Remember, God is infinitely greater than all your problems and trials, and you can trust that you're going to be okay in his powerful, loving hands.

PRAYER

Almighty God and loving Father, I am amazed when I think of how powerful and awesome you are, yet you love me so personally because I am your child. I trust you to take care of me according to your good plan, and I release control into your loving and powerful hands, knowing nothing is impossible for you.

16

Our Comforter

Give all your worries and cares to God, for he cares about you.

1 PETER 5:7

Howard Storm was a college professor and an ardent atheist, who by his own admission was unkind to his students, mocking those who believed in Jesus. After Howard's duodenum erupted on an art tour in France, he had a near-death experience. When he left his body, he found himself in a group of people who claimed they were there to help him but deceived him. Howard shared that he was led into the "outer darkness with weeping and gnashing of teeth," just as Jesus describes. In the midst of being eviscerated by horrible creatures, Howard cried out in desperation, "Jesus, save me!" Howard watched as a tiny point of light suddenly appeared, piercing the darkness, growing in brightness and size until it felt like the sun in all its brilliance was moving toward him.

Howard describes how arms then reached toward him out of the light, picked him up gently, and held him close like a parent who just found his long-lost child.

> This person of blinding glory loved me with overwhelming power. After what I had been through,

> to be completely known, accepted, and intensely loved by this beautiful God/man of light surpassed anything I had ever known or could possibly have imagined. I had called out to Jesus, and he came to rescue me. I cried and cried from joy, and the tears kept coming. Joy upon joy billowed through me. He held me and caressed me like a mother with her baby, like a father with his long-lost prodigal son. I cried all the tears of a lifetime of hopelessness and tears of shame over my unbelief. I cried all the tears of joy and salvation. I cried like a baby and couldn't stop crying. He held me close and stroked my back. We rose upward, gradually at first, and then like a rocket we shot out of that dark and detestable hell.[47]

No matter who you are or what you've done, God cares for you. He has always cared for you, even before you were aware of his presence. That's what Randy Kay discovered when he cried out to Jesus after a pulmonary embolism shut down his heart for thirty minutes. After walking and talking with Jesus in heaven, Randy was shown "vignettes" of his life, including memories that contained some very painful emotions when he was a child.

> All of these appearances were not visions, because visions are surreal or distant. I was actually there. I was in the hospital again, with my collapsed lungs, looking through the bars that kept me from falling out of the bed.
>
> "You were with me and I didn't even know it," I said.
>
> "Always, My beloved. You suffered as a child and I knew even then, how I would use your suffering."

> "I didn't blame You then, Lord, but I wanted someone to help me." I knew in that moment, that my compassion for those who suffer had come from my own understanding of suffering.
>
> "You only knew Me as a name and not as a Companion, beloved. But I knew you during all of your life."
>
> I felt Jesus tear up as I lay in that bed, and during the flood of times when I had gasped for breath. He viewed me as though I was the only person in the world. I felt Jesus's absolute devotion as though He cared only for me and nothing else. I also knew that He sees every person he has created, as though nothing else matters.[48]

....

God cares so much about his children, and he longs to comfort us through the challenges and difficulties of life. Even when we go through times of doubting his presence, God is still drawing near and will never leave our side.

God cares for us more than we could ever imagine, and he works through all the pains and sorrows of life to produce something beautiful for all who turn to him. As Isaiah 61:3 says, "To all who mourn in Israel, he will give a crown of beauty for ashes, a joyous blessing instead of mourning, festive praise instead of despair." One day, all our sorrows will turn to joy, but in our sorrows today, he is with us. God is "the Father of compassion and the God of all comfort, who comforts us in all our troubles, so that we can comfort those in any trouble with the comfort we ourselves receive from God" (2 Corinthians 1:3-4, NIV).

Even if you feel alone in your fear or grief, God is with you. You can lean into his loving arms. And remember, his care and comfort are not dependent on your good or bad actions—he cares for you because he loves you. So you can turn to him with the things that make you sad and go to him in those times that make you anxious. Cast all your cares on him because he cares for you more than you could ever imagine (1 Peter 5:7)! You can have confidence that he's restoring all things for good. Let his Spirit, who is called the Comforter, comfort you in all you're going through, and you'll find that same comfort will flow through you to others in need of the same.

PRAYER

Thank you, Lord, that you call yourself the Comforter. Your love and care for me is so great. I'm astounded that I'm so important to you. I cast all my cares and troubles on you today, asking you to bring the comfort and support I need to become a better person through it all.

17

God of All Nations

It is too small a thing for you to be my servant to restore the tribes of Jacob and bring back those of Israel I have kept. I will also make you a light for the Gentiles, that my salvation may reach to the ends of the earth.

ISAIAH 49:6, NIV

Marv Besteman was a retired bank president living in Byron Center, Michigan. After Marv had surgery for a rare pancreatic cancer at the University of Michigan hospital, something went wrong. Marv found himself beside his bed with two angels who escorted him to a spectacular world just outside heaven's gates. He noticed a diverse group of about thirty-five people with him outside the holy city of God.

> The smiles on everyone's faces seemed to say, "We made it! We finally, finally made it!" We were home at last, and we all knew it. Now, Byron Center, Michigan, is about as homogenous as any town can be, unfortunately. . . . Heaven was so different. Even the short line of about three dozen folks was a melting pot of colors, cultures, and costumes. I was wearing my normal "uniform," a golf shirt and khaki pants, the exact kind of outfit I would wear in my everyday life. The smiling people who stood in that line were from all over the world and wore all kinds of

> different clothing. I saw many different nationalities represented, including Scandinavian, Asian, African, and Middle Eastern. . . . A couple of the people I saw appeared to hail from primitive African tribes; they were wearing loose, flowing tribal gowns and toga-like garb with sandals on their feet. The man in front of me in line was Middle Eastern looking. . . . He wore a baggy, brown-colored caftan that looked like he had been sleeping in the dirt. Maybe he was a shepherd. . . . They all had big smiles on their faces.[49]

Rebecca Springer was a Christian living in America in the late 1800s. After dying from pneumonia, she wrote about having a heavenly experience, long before the term *near-death experience* was coined. In heaven, she and her deceased sister had the amazing experience of "flying" over a diverse group of villages where she gained unique insight into the God of all nations.

> As we passed onward, in looking down we began to see many suburban villages, . . . and the architecture of the buildings in many respects seemed quite different from our own. I suggested to my sister that we drop downward a little. On doing so, we soon realized what caused this apparent difference in the architecture and surroundings. Where our homes were situated, we were surrounded by people we had known and loved on earth, and of our own nationality. Many of these villages over which we were now passing we found were formed from what, to us, would be termed of foreign nations, and each village retained some of the peculiarities of its earth-life, and these, to us, were naturally unfamiliar. We recognized again the wisdom

> and goodness of the Father in thus allowing friends of the same nationality to be located near each other in Heaven, as on earth.
>
> As we still drifted onward, in passing over an exquisitely beautiful valley, between low hills of the most enchanting verdure, we saw a group of people seated upon the ground in a semicircle. They seemed to be hundreds in number, and in their midst a man was standing who, apparently, was talking to them. . . . "Let us go nearer, and hear, if possible, what he is saying, and see who these people are." Upon doing this we found the people to resemble in a great measure our own Indian tribes [Native Americans]; their dress, in a manner corresponding to that worn upon earth, though so etherealized as to be surpassingly beautiful. But the dusky faces and the long black hair still remained.

Surprised to see this person teaching the gathered crowd, Rebecca exclaimed, "Why, he is a missionary!" Rebecca mentioned that in heaven, whenever a surprise presented itself, someone was always there to enlighten her. She heard a male voice reply:

> "Yes, you are right. This is a missionary who gave his life . . . working for them and enlightening those who sat in darkness, with the result, as you see before you, of bringing hundreds into the kingdom of the Master. But, as you will naturally suppose, they have much to learn, and here he still gathers them about him, and day by day leads them higher and higher into the blessed life." "Are there many such," I asked, "doing

> this work in this beautiful realm?" "Many hundreds," he said. "To these poor minds, unenlightened as they were when they first came, Heaven is as beautiful and happy a place as it is to any who have ascended higher, simply because we can enjoy only in the capacity to which our souls can reach. There are none of us who have not much yet to learn of this wonderful country."[50]

....

God is the God of all nations. God does not love any one group of people more or less than another. In fact, God's image is most fully reflected in all of humanity combined. All that God has done for one of us, God has done for all of us; and from the beginning, God's great plan has included every nationality. Four thousand years ago, he said to Abraham and Sarah, "I will make you into a great nation. . . . And *all peoples on earth* will be blessed through you" (Genesis 12:2-3, NIV, emphasis added).

The God of the Bible is the only deity described in history who claims to speak to all the nations and has a plan for all the nations. Through the Jewish prophets, God foretold the Messiah who "will bring justice to the nations" (Isaiah 42:1). And the risen Jesus told his disciples, "It was written long ago that the Messiah would suffer and die and rise from the dead on the third day. . . . [And] that this message would be proclaimed in the authority of his name to all the nations, beginning in Jerusalem: 'There is forgiveness of sins for all who repent'" (Luke 24:46-47).

God loves all people from every nation and culture, and he sent Jesus to the world so that every person on earth could experience the wonders of his love, forgiveness, and grace. God made the ultimate sacrifice for the sake of humanity, and he wants us to be willing to make sacrifices to share his love and compassion with others. If you have received the eternal, priceless gift of knowing Jesus as your personal Savior, you can show your gratitude by sharing the good news with those who haven't yet experienced his magnificent love.

It's humbling to realize we are part of God's grand plan to help people all over the world know and follow Jesus! And the more we continue to grow and help others grow in the love and understanding of God while here on earth, the greater capacity we will all have to experience the wonders of God one day in heaven. Remember, there is no greater position on earth than serving as God's ambassador, sharing his love and forgiveness with all those who are still seeking. Take some time now to think of people you know who need to hear this good news. People of every nation, tribe, and language are longing to know of God's mercy and grace offered through Jesus, and God has appointed you to tell them.

PRAYER

God of all nations, I see how much your heart and desire has always been for your children of all nations to come home to you. Help me love the nations like you do, and give me courage to tell others about you and all you've done for them.

18

Motherly Love

As a mother comforts her child, so will I comfort you.

ISAIAH 66:13, NIV

Micki had lost all hope. She believed in Jesus, but her husband was divorcing her, and she found herself in despair to the point of death after taking too many antidepressants. During her near-death experience, Micki saw a brilliant light shining down from a throne high above her, and she knew this was God. She also found herself embraced by the tender, nurturing love of the presence of Jesus.

> I turned, . . . and there stood Jesus Christ. . . . I ran to him and wrapped my arms around his feet, kissing his feet, and telling him how much I loved him. His arms came down and he held my head close to him as I cried hard.
>
> God then spoke mentally to me and told me how much he loved me . . . and told me to go back; "your time has not yet come." I pleaded with him and fell to my knees. . . . I was crying and begging so loud that I suddenly felt God's arms come down . . . and he lifted me off my feet and cradled me as a mother cradles her

> baby against her breast. He rocked me and held me in his arms.[51]

God gently put Micki back on her feet and told her she had to go back because children were going to be born to her. The doctors had told her she could never have children. When she opened her eyes, her husband was on his knees praying that God would bring her back to him. Micki's marriage was healed, and she did have children just as God had promised.

Jeff also experienced God's tender care during his NDE. Jeff was in a deep trench working on a water well, when a dump truck's worth of wet, heavy shale and mud collapsed on him, suffocating him as he cried out to his coworker for help. He then found himself at the throne of God. Jeff recalls,

> So much love. Pure divine love around everything everywhere. I was totally engulfed in it. I saw things I can't even begin to describe. The awe factor was way off the charts. . . . I immediately hit the floor face down saying, "I am not worthy to be here. I should not be here" over and over again. I was before the Holy Trinity. I couldn't look at it. It was so blindingly bright. . . . When I came to, I was being cradled in this huge energy-like ball that felt endless and was truly feminine in nature. Like the best-est mom in all the universe.[52]

....

Although God is described as a heavenly Father, he also likens himself to a loving mother throughout Scripture. Like the perfect mother's love, God's love is selfless, nurturing, kind, patient, compassionate, merciful, loyal, protective, and supportive. God compares himself to a nursing mother who never abandons her child, no matter what. This is how God feels for all of us. When his people said, "The Lord has deserted us; the Lord has forgotten us," God responded through the prophet Isaiah: "Never! Can a mother forget her nursing child? Can she feel no love for the child she has borne? But even if that were possible, I would not forget you! See, I have written your name on the palms of my hands" (Isaiah 49:14-16).

An exemplary mother's love has no boundaries and gives from a bottomless well of love and devotion. She always sees the potential of who we can be and believes the best. She encourages us to be brave, yet she is there to watch over us and catch us when we fall. God's maternal love is the same: "Like an eagle that rouses her chicks and hovers over her young, so he spread his wings to take them up and carried them safely on his pinions" (Deuteronomy 32:11).

God cares for us so deeply that he has our names permanently inscribed on his hands. Like a loving mother, he is always thinking of us and holding us close in his heart. Jesus used another maternal image to describe his motherly love: He said to those in Jerusalem who had rejected him, "How often I have wanted to gather your children together as a hen protects her chicks beneath her wings, but you wouldn't let me" (Luke 13:34). He feels this same way about all of us, desiring to protect us like a good mother, yet respecting our choices if we reject his love. He is always ready to forgive and welcome us back no matter what.

God's comforting and compassionate presence is always there for you. God will walk before you when you need a guide, beside you when you need a friend, and behind you when you need an encourager. You can trust in his loyalty and devotion.

Take a moment now to focus on the nurturing, selfless, and loyal maternal love that God has for you.

Whether you have a loving earthly mother or not, let God's perfect love bring you peace and courage to face whatever challenges come your way. God is always there for you, will always support you, and will never reject you. You are forever his beloved child.

PRAYER

Dear God, thank you for your strong, nurturing, maternal care for me. You love me like a nursing mother loves her child and will always hold me close. Help me to remember that I am and will always be loved and cherished by you.

19

The Intimacy of God

O God, you are my God; I earnestly search for you.
My soul thirsts for you; my whole body longs for you. . . .
Your unfailing love is better than life itself; how I praise you!

PSALM 63:1, 3

Cedric Pisegna turned away from his faith during college, focusing on partying and women. At age twenty, Cedric got his girlfriend pregnant, and they chose to abort the baby. For months following, guilt overwhelmed him, and a year after the abortion, he cried out to God in repentance.

Then one night in his sleep, Cedric found himself leaving his body and, in a hyper-vivid reality, standing before God's throne. When talking about his near-death experience, Cedric describes the surprising intimacy he felt in God's presence:

> I thought, *Oh, no*, because I knew I was not ready to come before God. . . . Suddenly, I found myself in the presence of God, standing before the Throne. The only way to describe it was a living luminescent light that embraced me.[53]
>
> God's love for me was intensely personal. I sensed that I was known and loved even before I was born into this world. His love was unconditional. God's care and affection for me were not conditioned

> on my goodness; rather, there was such powerful, pulsating goodness radiating from God that it was overwhelming. . . . God's love is an energetic passion. God's love is affectionate. It is very intimate and personal. I realized that not only did God love me; he was *in love with me*! What I mean is that he knew me through and through and still had his heart set upon me. . . . I was overwhelmed with the intensity and intimacy of God's love. God is obsessed with us! Agape love was displayed through Jesus in his willingness to be tortured on the Cross. True love is sacrificial and willing to suffer. This love is inexhaustible, indefatigable. . . . There was a wonderful oneness with God. I had a deep personal union of which marriage is but a symbol.[54]

After Cedric's profound experience of the passionate, intimate love God has for him, his life completely turned around. He dedicated the rest of his life to sharing the Passion of Jesus' redeeming work of the cross with others as a Catholic Passionist priest.

Wayne Fowler is an aerospace engineer and lawyer in Australia who came to faith in Jesus one week before he suffered a massive heart attack. He describes his intense, intimate encounter with God during his NDE as if he were experiencing it again in real time.

> Into his presence, brighter than ten thousand suns—and I'm transfixed! It is awesomely beautiful. And I can see down into this light. At the center is the form of a man, arms outstretched towards me, like to welcome me and to hug me. At that moment, I

> entered. I merged with the light, and the light merged with me. Like when Jesus said, I am in you, and you in me [John 17:21]. I was like a glass container being filled up, filled up, filled up with him. And I was experiencing the most ecstatic love. It was bliss beyond belief, rapture beyond reason, ecstasy beyond explanation—love times a billion—but our word *love* fails so badly. Imagine every loving relationship combined all together, then blow them up billions of times all of that![55]

. . . .

Upon reading these experiences by those who have felt God's exhilarating presence, it can seem far out and unfathomable that God, our Creator, would desire such intimacy and oneness uniquely with each of us. Yet it is true! Jesus prayed for this on the night before his crucifixion: "I pray that they will all be one, just as you and I are one—as you are in me, Father, and I am in you. And may they be in us" (John 17:21).

We don't need to hide anything from God because he already knows us inside and out. Instead, we can walk in full transparency with him, talking over everything, even the shameful things we don't want to expose. This is the kind of vulnerability and intimacy God wants with us. We are already acceptable, worthy, lovable, and complete in God's sight because God's passion made us that way—by the cross.

No one on earth could love you more deeply and personally than God already loves you! Today, focus on receiving this intimate love from God. Talk vulnerably with him about everything on your heart and receive his promise to draw close to you. Listen in your heart for his tender words spoken uniquely to you. You will feel the difference it makes in your life as you realize that you are fully loved and valued by the one who loves you most.

PRAYER

Heavenly Father, your passionate love for me is so great—beyond anything I have ever or could ever experience here on earth! Help me to draw close to you in the intimate, loving relationship you desire with me, remaining open and honest with you every moment of every day, receiving your words of tender love.

20

God Hears You

When they cried out to you again, you heard from heaven, and in your compassion you delivered them time after time.

NEHEMIAH 9:28, NIV

Steve Kang, a former Buddhist, got into drugs during college. He smoked a "death bowl," consisting of marijuana mixed with many powerful psychedelic drugs. This led him into a suicide attempt that resulted in a terrifying near-death experience, where Steve reports that Jesus dramatically came to save him from hell. He miraculously survived. Steve believes this happened because his mother, a Buddhist at that time, turned to her Christian friend to pray to Jesus with her for Steve's recovery. Her friend brought eight more people to join them in the ICU to pray to Jesus and intercede for Steve. Today, Steve's mother is a devoted follower of Jesus, and Steve is now a pastor. They both know beyond a shadow of a doubt that prayer has immense power and can move the hand of God.[56]

Likewise, God honored the prayers of Ian McCormack's mother. As Ian was thousands of miles from home dying from multiple box jellyfish stings, God awakened his mother in the middle of the night to pray for Ian, and she obeyed the prompting. At the same time, Ian had a vision of his mother telling him to pray the Lord's Prayer—a prayer she had taught him as a child. Ian, now a Christian minister, says that during his NDE, Jesus showed him that these prayers are what moved the hand of God to rescue him, as he turned to Jesus during his last breaths.[57]

Ivan Tuttle also credits his mother's prayers for saving his life. At age twenty-six, Ivan found himself in a hellish NDE after partying and consuming drugs for days. Then, he said,

> I heard a voice like a mighty roar of thunder that said, "It is not his time yet. His mother has been praying for him since he was a little boy. You must release him now; I made a promise!" The voice said my mother had prayed over twenty-eight thousand times for me, and it was her faithful prayers that saved me.[58]

During Dr. Gary Wood's NDE after a car accident, he witnessed how valuable our prayers are to God. In heaven, he was led to the throne of God by his deceased childhood friend, John. Gary shares what he saw:

> I saw angels carrying golden bowls filled with a liquid substance. I asked John what it was, and he told me it was the tears of the saints below. Every time a child of God prays so earnestly that a teardrop falls, an angel is there to catch that tear and deliver it to God. The tears are stored in golden bowls at the base of God's throne. I saw other angels carrying golden vials filled with a vaporlike substance. I asked the angels what it was, and they replied, "It is the praises of the people on earth presented to God as sweet-smelling incense."[59]

....

God loves to hear our prayers and lighten our burdens. In fact, every tear, struggle, petition, desire, or heartache we bring to God in prayer is valuable and significant to him. Psalm 56:8 beautifully expresses how much God values our hearts' cries: "You keep track of all my sorrows. You have collected all my tears in your bottle. You have recorded each one in your book." God holds our tears as his precious treasures when we call out to him in prayer through the valleys of life.

Our prayers are not only important to God, but they are substantial and effective, and they can make a powerful difference in the world. Our prayers set things in motion, including the angels of God. Even though we may not always see how our intercessions play out as God works with each person's free will, we can have assurance that our prayers for others have profound effects. James 5:16 says, "The earnest prayer of a righteous person has great power and produces wonderful results."

If you are a parent, you may be praying for your child now or have been for a very long time. Don't give up, even if it seems like your prayers aren't making a difference or nothing is changing. Keep praying with a steadfast heart—God is moving in ways you don't see yet, but you will one day! He is working in your child's life for the good, and he promises that you can trust him and his timing. The persistent prayers of a parent are special to God, and you can find comfort in knowing that they matter—a lot.

In this moment, rest assured that your prayers are never lost, and God pays attention to each one. You can trust in his unwavering faithfulness and goodness to work through them for his Kingdom purposes in you, your loved ones, and the world. Take some time today to bring your concerns to him; he is always ready to listen. Remember, you are his cherished child, and he cares about what is on your heart. You can trust that he will respond in his perfect timing, and you will receive what you need most from your good Father.

PRAYER

Dear heavenly Father, thank you for listening to my heart's cry and every concern. I know that you are working through my prayers, even though I may not see the outcome yet. Help me to persevere in prayer, trusting that you will answer in your perfect timing for my good and the good of my loved ones.

21

Gracious Gift-Giver

So if you sinful people know how to give good gifts to your children, how much more will your heavenly Father give good gifts to those who ask him.

MATTHEW 7:11

Erica McKenzie was bullied as a child. After years of battling an eating disorder and addiction to diet pills, Erica's heart failed. During Erica's near-death experience, she felt like a child in the arms of a safe, loving Father. While she was with God, he began to teach Erica about the importance of the gifts God's Spirit gives to each one of us, and how we are to receive and cultivate them for the good of humanity.

> I went up and up, and I knew I was going to Heaven. It seemed as if I rose infinitely past the stars and farther into the all-encompassing light until I had finally reached the end of the tunnel. Once there, the most all-encompassing feeling of love overwhelmed me. . . .
>
> While I could not see a physical image, I distinguished this brilliant Presence as the voice I had heard all my life. . . . It was God.[60]
>
> He brought me close to Him like a parent about to tell a child a story. We stood together with our backs towards Heaven and looked out at the stars. . . .

To my right . . . were the most amazing, multidimensional shelves. The shelves reached high into the stars until I could no longer see the tops of them. . . . On the shelves appeared gifts, presents, like those we give and receive at Christmas. There were so many gifts on all of the shelves that they filled each and every space available. But not one gift looked like the other. . . .

God said, "When you are born, I give each of you gifts. When you were born, Erica, I gave you the gift of patience and the gift of beauty." Immediately I thought, "Oh no, God, that can't be right!" I recalled the kids in school. If I were truly beautiful, I wouldn't have been judged. . . . He so lovingly corrected me by saying telepathically, "Erica, I gave you the gift of patience, and I gave you the gift of beauty." God added, "In life, I have more gifts for each and every one of you. All you have to do is ask, and then be prepared to be quiet and listen, to be able to receive these gifts."

Sometimes it's hard to see the gifts we possess. I thought of my gift of beauty and realized how impossible it was for me to see it in myself because I looked to mankind for my value instead of God. . . . It took dying to make me realize that my uniqueness was my value, and my value was my contribution on this Earthly Journey. As we stood together in silence, God filled me with the knowledge that it was important to share these lessons with others. . . . I understood it's never about one person using their gifts or uniqueness alone. Rather, it is God's plan for us to embrace our uniqueness and come together to embrace and empower each other.[61]

. . . .

Scripture teaches that God is a gift-giver. How blessed we are to each receive handpicked gifts from our heavenly Father! And these gifts are worth far more than anything money can buy. The spiritual gifts we've been given to develop and express, uniquely reflect God's heart and his image to the world. When used as God intended, they have the capacity to serve the Kingdom of God in ways that ripple across humanity.

Sometimes people shy away from developing their gifts, and many don't even recognize they have them. Without a doubt, forces in the world can cause us to feel insecure and unworthy in the very ways God has gifted us. But just like a good parent wants to give gifts to their children, God wants to give gifts to you. And these gifts will be right in line with the way he has wired you. In 1 Corinthians 12:4-7, the apostle Paul writes, "There are different kinds of spiritual gifts, but the same Spirit is the source of them all. There are different kinds of service, but we serve the same Lord. God works in different ways, but it is the same God who does the work in all of us. A spiritual gift is given to each of us so we can help each other."

Maybe you have a spiritual gift of hospitality and enjoy welcoming others into your life and home. Maybe you have a gift of encouragement and have the right words to say to build someone else up at just the right time. Perhaps you have gifts of mercy, leadership, serving, or words of knowledge to help people. In Scripture, 1 Corinthians 12 and Romans 12 reveal many of the gifts and how to view them in context with others. Take some time to reflect on these passages and ask God to help you discern what gifts he has given to you.

In gratitude to God for your gifts, do your best to cultivate them and use them in community with others. By doing so, you are reflecting the gift-giver and giving God glory. Today, take time to reflect on your God-given gifts and actively work to develop them or put them into action, using your talents to bring honor to him.

PRAYER

Dear Father, thank you for the spiritual gifts you have given me. Help me to discover them and develop them in ways that reflect you and shine your love to the world. Show me how you want me to use my gifts in community with others.

22

Jesus, Our Brother

It was only right that [God] should make Jesus, through his suffering, a perfect leader, fit to bring them into their salvation. So now Jesus and the ones he makes holy have the same Father. That is why Jesus is not ashamed to call them his brothers and sisters. For he said to God, "I will proclaim your name to my brothers and sisters."

HEBREWS 2:10-12

While undergoing minor laparoscopic surgery for fertility issues, Julie had internal bleeding and found herself rushed to the ICU of a San Antonio hospital. For a week, doctors worked to no avail to stop the bleeding, and finally, Julie's organs shut down. She found herself in the presence of Jesus near the river of life during her near-death experience. There, she gained new understanding of Jesus as her loving older brother.

> We then walked over next to the river, then Jesus took both my hands, turning my palms upward. While holding my hands, he said, "I want you to remember something. You are of a royal lineage. You are a child of God. The Most High God. You live in the world but are not of the world. Your rightful place is in Heaven with the Father."
>
> I said, "Yes, I understand." The whole while he was telling me this, I felt like I was the most precious, most

loved, most beloved person in existence. Next, I asked, "Just what is your relationship to me?"

Jesus said, "I am your brother."

I said, "I know that's what the Bible says, so it's true then?"

Jesus said, "Yes, I am your brother. We have the same blood running through our veins. I will never leave you or forsake you. I will always be there for you. Never ever forget who you are."[62]

Lead software engineer Jeremy[**] had a couple glasses of wine that reacted adversely with medication he had taken, and he stopped breathing. During his NDE, Jeremy found himself in a beautiful garden setting, just outside what seemed like a waiting room. After getting a tour of heaven's beauty, he had another realization:

> I went back to the waiting room. Just after we got back, one of the people in the waiting room introduced me to my "brother." My "brother" was just walking in from the courtyard area. I never understood this part until a few months ago because I do not recognize this person as my biological brother. When I looked at my "brother," I thought to myself that he isn't my brother, and everyone could tell that I was thinking this. I could tell they all knew this man was my "brother." Also since I knew this "brother" of mine was the mediator between me and God, he was certainly not my biological brother. . . . Recently, I read a verse in the New Testament about Jesus saying,

---

** Jeremy is a pseudonym.

> "Who are my brothers . . . whoever follows my Father is my brother." Now, when I think about this, it brings tears of joy to me, and I don't cry often.[63]

....

Jesus, the Son of God, calls himself our brother. The fact that he lowered himself, coming from heaven to earth to become one of us—a brother, a confidant, a friend—is astounding!

As our brother, Jesus understands everything we go through because he has experienced it all himself. He really does know what life is like as a human being on this side of heaven. Hebrews 2:17-18 says, "It was necessary for him to be made in every respect like us, his brothers and sisters, so that he could be our merciful and faithful High Priest before God. Then he could offer a sacrifice that would take away the sins of the people. Since he himself has gone through suffering and testing, he is able to help us when we are being tested."

Jesus fully understands what you're going through and wants to help you as you lean on him. You can find comfort in knowing that just like you, he has been through earthly temptations, testing, and suffering, and he can offer genuine support in your time of need. Your brother, Jesus, loves you unconditionally, understands you completely, has your back, and will always be there for you. Today, imagine Jesus as your loving, protective brother and best friend, and confide in him all that is on your heart.

PRAYER

Jesus, thank you for becoming one of us, so that we can relate to you like a close, protective brother who understands. You can relate when I'm tempted, struggling, and hurting. I can go to you with it all because you went through it all. Help me walk with you daily and trust you with everything, because you truly understand.

23

The Holy Spirit

And I will ask the Father, and he will give you another Advocate, who will never leave you. He is the Holy Spirit, who leads into all truth. . . . You know him, because he lives with you now and later will be in you. . . . When the Father sends the Advocate as my representative—that is, the Holy Spirit—he will teach you everything and will remind you of everything I have told you. I am leaving you with a gift—peace of mind and heart.

JOHN 14:16-17, 26-27

Many people who have had a near-death experience say they did not "see" the Holy Spirit in heaven, but they realized that the Holy Spirit is God's presence with us, given to lead and guide us.

Twelve-year-old Susanne Seymoure and her family were skiing together in the Poconos when Susanne's scarf got caught in the tow rope, resulting in a tragic accident leading to certain death. Miraculously, Susanne revived. Prior to the accident, Susanne knew nothing about the Bible or the triune nature of God; but during her near-death experience, she found herself taken by Jesus to a place where she experienced the splendor of Almighty God as one with Jesus, and afterward Jesus showed her an image of his Holy Spirit:

> Jesus brought me back to the scene of the accident, and he stayed with me as I went back into my body. He gave

> me a mental picture of a bird, like a dove with wings open, and he pointed to my chest, and it's like he put a dove in my chest and said, "I will always be with you." And I realized coming back that God is always with us, and he let me know his Spirit is for everyone, but not everyone receives him or accesses his Spirit's availability. But we don't ever have to be alone—he wants us to know he's always with us to love and guide us.[64]

After being guided by Jesus to the throne of God the Father during his own NDE, Father Cedric Pisegna realized the Holy Spirit is God's presence with him today.

> I experienced the Holy Spirit when I came back. The same glory I felt in God the Father's presence I also felt, but to a much lesser degree, in prayer and everyday life. Remember what Jesus said, "Behold, I stand at the door and knock. If anyone hears my voice and opens the door, I will come in to him and eat with him, and he with me" (Revelation 3:20, ESV). I believe that the door talked about is the portal to eternity residing in our heart. . . . Opening that door takes work and discipline and grace. Usually, we are far from it, unaware and living in sensuality and carnality. But if we can slow down and get centered, we can begin to transcend time itself and enter the place of rest, God's glorious presence within us.[65]

When Dean Braxton died of sepsis, he saw Jesus and the Father, separate and yet one. Dean also experienced the Holy Spirit as God's presence inside his own spirit, both in heaven and after he returned to earth.

> When I got there [to Heaven] the Holy Spirit was on the inside of me. . . . He stayed with me. . . . Jesus said, "I'll never leave you." When I'm here on the planet, he's still with me that close. . . . I came to understand it's not about a feeling. When he said he's with you, he entered in, whether you feel it or not. We have to go by what he says, not what we think or feel. So I tell people, he's very close to you. How much closer can he get? He's on the inside of you![66]

. . . .

The most powerful gift believers have been given is the Holy Spirit—God's presence within us. This can seem strange to think about, and even hard to comprehend fully. But learning how to go through life with the Spirit's guidance and empowerment is the most critical thing we can do for our lives.

Many believers are unaware of the power and encouragement that lies within them through the Spirit, and this can hold them back from experiencing the fullness of God's love and the life he desires for them. All believers have the Holy Spirit available: "When you believed in Christ, he identified you as his own by giving you the Holy Spirit" (Ephesians 1:13) to dwell in you, pour his love into your heart, and help you endure by giving strength on which to stand (see John 14:16-17, 26-27). Though the Holy Spirit is in every believer, we must daily choose if we will "be filled with the Holy Spirit" (Ephesians 5:18). The Holy Spirit will fill your mind and guide you as you willingly listen and obey those quiet thoughts that prompt you to speak or act in alignment with God's will.

Before Jesus ascended to heaven, he promised his disciples that his Father would send the Holy Spirit, who would be his presence in the heart of every believer. The Spirit would bring peace to their minds and hearts. Think about the role the Holy Spirit has in your life. Are you allowing the Spirit to give you peace? When anxious thoughts enter your mind, focus on turning your worries into prayers. Ask the Holy Spirit to give you peace and assurance that God can work all things for your good as you set your mind on Jesus and follow his leading.

The Holy Spirit wants to comfort and soothe your heart, and as God's child, you can find refuge and strength in the Spirit's presence. Take a moment now to acknowledge the Holy Spirit and release your worries and burdens into God's safe hands. Open your heart to receive the peace God's Spirit promises to give you—mentally, emotionally, and spiritually. The Holy Spirit is your secret weapon! As you listen and respond to the Holy Spirit's guiding promptings, you will experience a wonderful difference in your life.

PRAYER

Dear God, thank you for the gift of your Spirit to live in me and actively guide me. Help me to receive the wisdom, love, and peace you want to give me as I lean on you. Holy Spirit, I trust your guidance in my life.

24

Our Redeemer

Christ redeemed us from the curse of the law by becoming a curse for us.

GALATIANS 3:13, NIV

Dr. Rajiv Parti was an anesthesiologist who thought near-death experiences were merely psychosis. He grew up in India as a Hindu but lost all belief in God, heaven, and hell when he became a medical doctor. All that changed when his intestines ruptured and, during emergency surgery, he had his own NDE. When he first found himself in a hellish experience, *Naraka*, the Hindi word for hell, came to his mind. He thought, *What is my karma?*[67] Then he heard a voice answer:

> "You have lived a very loveless life." I had been mean. I wanted to get ahead in life no matter what it cost me. If I had to step on others' toes, I did not mind doing that. And I was not good to my patients. . . . A seventy-year-old lady came to my office for arthritis medicine. She wanted to talk to me because her husband was dying of lung cancer. . . . [But] I just wrote the prescription in two minutes and walked away. I treated her like a disease, . . . not as a human being.[68]

Rajiv felt shame as he thought about these things. Additionally, his father had been very abusive toward him growing up, and Rajiv had begun to treat his own sons the same way.

> There appeared to be no way out, but I prayed for one anyway. "My God, give me another chance." . . . I was praying and had repentance, and who showed up was my father.[69] "Don't pass the anger to your sons," he said.[70]

Afterward, Rajiv was taken by two angels to a God of brilliant light and love, who gave him a life review showing him what needed to change when he returned to earth. Rajiv later asked this God of light, "Who are you?" He answered, "I am Jesus, your savior."[71] After his NDE, Rajiv did break the generational patterns of abuse and addiction as he followed Jesus.

Howard Storm also grew up with a horribly abusive father. As a result, he hardened his heart and became a mean, unfaithful, atheistic professor who lived for himself. When Howard's duodenum ruptured while he was in France, he died and found himself in a hellish place similar to the one Rajiv experienced. Howard cried out to Jesus, and a brilliant light appeared and took him out of the darkness. As Jesus tenderly held him, he was given a life review.

> So, what I learned in my life review was that the relationship with my father—I had participated in the breakdown of that relationship as much as he did. He was not a good father to me, and I resented it, and I was angry at him. So, I did everything I could—subconsciously and sometimes consciously—to be as rebellious and as cold-hearted towards him as possible, which only aggravated him more and made him more

> of a hostile father. So, the things that I had seen in my life where I was the victim and everybody else was the bad guy, I came to find out was a two-way street. We were both playing this game. . . . God created me to love God and love my fellow people, including, myself. And, because I did not have the love of God, I did not have any self-love. All of the striving was to prove my worth to the world, which you can never do, . . . because the thing that we crave in our hearts is to be fully known and to be loved for who we are, which only God can give us. Our parents can't give it, our spouses can't give it, nobody can give it except God. And, when you have that love of God, you don't have to prove your worth.[72]

Howard realized that Jesus wanted him to take responsibility to love even those who feel like enemies. Howard came back to earth determined to break the cycle of abuse, unfaithfulness, and self-centeredness with Jesus' help. He would be the first to tell you he's not perfect; but he walks humbly with God who is healing him, and today Howard and his father have healed their relationship. God is redeeming and restoring what generational sin destroyed.

....

It is easy to see that our world is broken and marred with the effects of evil and sin, and generation after generation has suffered the consequences of choices made before them. This is one of the spiritual laws God told Moses: "I lay the sins of the parents upon their children; the entire family is affected—even children in the third and fourth generations of those who reject me. But I lavish unfailing love for a thousand generations on those who love me and obey my commands" (Exodus 20:5-6). God's spiritual laws warn us that when we persistently go against God's will and ways, the consequences pass down.

But we can break the stronghold that evil has attempted to claim over our lives from generations before us. God's redemptive love will shine into the darkness of the past that has held families captive. Jesus promised, "If you hold to my teaching, . . . you will know the truth, and the truth will set you free" (John 8:31-32, NIV).

God is a redeemer. To redeem means to buy back or restore. "'With everlasting kindness I will have compassion on you,' says the LORD your Redeemer" (Isaiah 54:8, NIV). If you have experienced generational sin passing down, be assured that Jesus paid a steep price to redeem you from those long-held chains. And God will honor the courageous effort you put forth to live your life differently than what has been passed down to you. Remember, Jesus has already paid to forgive you and redeem you from the curse of generational sin, and by the leadership of his Spirit and obeying his teachings, you *can* break free!

You can start now—break the chains and begin blessing your children and your children's children. Today, make the decision to turn from any generational stronghold that still has a grip on you. With God's help, you can be free, and you can set future generations free! From your obedience, God promises to lavish his unfailing love on a thousand generations to follow.

PRAYER

Mighty God, show me any strongholds of past generations that bind me, and I will turn from them. Redeem my past with your unfailing love. Give me courage to be obedient to you, following your will and ways daily, so I can break the chains that hold me back, and thank you for blessing the generations after me with your faithful love.

25

Our Good Father

I thought to myself, "I would love to treat you as my own children!" I wanted nothing more than to give you this beautiful land—the finest possession in the world. I looked forward to your calling me "Father," and I wanted you never to turn from me.

JEREMIAH 3:19

"My first memory is of God," Heidi Barr recalls. "He was present at my bedside for as long as I can remember." Heidi didn't experience a loving father in her home. Her father was abusive and unloving, a Jewish atheist who taught Heidi there was no God, Jesus was a hoax, and her life was meaningless. Yet somehow, as a child, she knew the truth. Heidi knew she was loved by God, and she prayed to God every night.

> My mom didn't feel beautiful; she didn't feel valued, and that contributed . . . to my belief that I was unloved, except in the eyes of God. He loved me. I knew this even as a child. My *real Father* [in Heaven] loved me. Knowing I had a real Father saved my life many times. Did God sit at my bedside, at the head of my bed? Yes, yes, he did. How do I know? I clearly remember *knowing* he was there. I had a powerful sense that he sat right next to me, listening to my childish hopes and fears, my dreams. He paid attention

> to my little complaints when some injustice had been done. He also rocked me to sleep. Sounds strange, doesn't it? God rocked me to sleep every single night. In truth it was Jesus, but I didn't know it at the time. And of course, Jesus and God are one and the same, yet different—and that is a concept I will leave for the theologians.[73]

At sixteen, Heidi was crushed to death under her horse and found herself up in the air with Jesus. She instantly knew he was the God to whom she had prayed every night, and she saw his tender, fatherly love.

> I later learned, during my life review, it was Jesus who had done this for me. I saw him there, exactly as I pictured him, sitting at the head of my bed, right beside my pillow, his head inclined toward me as he listened. And when he felt it was time for me to sleep, he himself surrounded me with his own light and rocked me.[74]

Jesus then took Heidi into the infinite light of God, where she found herself cuddled up as if on the Father's lap.

> Jesus took me directly into the light, and I found myself sitting on God's lap—God the Father, but yes, Jesus too. They were one and the same, yet separate, but again, still one. See how difficult this is to explain? So, there I was, sitting on God's lap, kicking my legs like a little girl. I had my arms wrapped around his waist. I buried my face in his chest. Talk about a perfect love. . . . Love incarnate. All love. Every single

> smidge of love in existence. That was God. He had his arms around me too. He held me tight. And he's a big God. I was like a toddler sitting on her father's lap. . . . I was humbled, but I felt no fear, only awe in the truest sense of the word. I had come home to my real Father. He loved me. He loved me with all the love in the universe. What my [earthly] dad had told me wasn't true. It was a lie. My life was not less significant than the most microscopic speck of dust in the universe. My life had significance to God. God knew me. God comforted me. God accepted me. God loved me. God filled every single corner of me. He filled my heart. I never wanted to leave him.[75]

....

God has given all of us earthly fathers who are meant to reflect the protection, comfort, acceptance, and love of our heavenly Father. However, no father can do this perfectly. Some may fail in small ways while others may fail in terrible, traumatic ways. But just as Heidi came to realize, we all have a perfect Father who is willing to help us take the good things that our earthly fathers may have modeled and understand that God is an even better Father. He also wants to heal the father-wounds, where our dads did not follow God's will and hurt us, by reminding us of the truth of his great protective, caring, and comforting love. This love has always held your true worth and value like a special treasure in his heart.

Your heavenly Father sees you as his perfect child, flawlessly created and loved. He takes immense delight in your love and affection toward him and wants you to know that he is a good, good Father who always has your best interests at heart.

He desires you to listen to his voice, speaking words of belief, encouragement, and great worth into your identity. As the one who formed you in your mother's womb and has watched over you since, he knows you better than anyone else. He longs to take your hand and tenderly guide you, just like any loving father would.

Take some time today to reflect on the positive qualities of your earthly dad that demonstrate the heart of a good father, and thank your heavenly Father for this example. And where your dad failed to reflect God's fatherly heart, ask God to reveal the truth to your soul today. It can be difficult to receive and believe positive words of affirmation if you were constantly criticized, but choose to trust your heavenly Father. Listen to his encouraging, comforting, protecting, and endearing words that show how much you mean to him, and let his words of truth replace the hurtful words of the past. Remember, God is your heavenly Father, and you are his beloved child.

PRAYER

Father in heaven, I believe that you are a good Father. Help me to internalize how much you care for me, and give me confidence to find my true identity and security in you. Thank you for loving me unconditionally and perfectly.

26

God of Majesty and Strength

Tell everyone about God's power. His majesty shines down on Israel; his strength is mighty in the heavens. God is awesome in his sanctuary. The God of Israel gives power and strength to his people. Praise be to God!

PSALM 68:34-35

While Dean Braxton's body lay dead in the hospital after all his organs shut down from sepsis, Dean's spirit felt the awe-inspiring magnificence and creative power of God on his throne in exhilarating ways:

> No matter where I went in Heaven, God was there. I could also look to the throne—it's the center of everything—but no matter how far I was from the locale of the throne, I could look at him and be up next to him from anywhere. And I always felt he was there with me. The focal point was the Father, and all else surrounds him. . . . The glory of God is shining out of everything, so it kind of looks translucent. The glass sea is different; it's blue but mingled with fire, and it's changing and growing greater and greater. The whole realm of the Father was so beautiful and intense; everything was like beautiful artwork growing in intensity. God's creative power makes everything increasingly more and more beautiful in Heaven.

> Just as everything on the earth is deteriorating and falling apart, everything in Heaven is growing and getting better—they're moving in opposite directions. But the Father held the attention fully. It was just overwhelming wonder. . . . In Heaven, I experienced "the fear of the Lord" [described] in Scripture. It is a sense of awe and respect.[76]

Richard Sigmund, whose near-death experience followed a terrible car accident, recalls,

> [The throne area] was wider and higher than I could even imagine—hundreds of miles, with massive arches and pillars. Everything in Heaven comes out of the throne. . . . As I got nearer to it, the air became electrically charged with the power and presence of God. . . . The closer I got to the throne, the more everything became transparent. Everything is absolutely transparent, with purity closest to God. I saw Jesus walk up to the throne and disappear into the enfolding fire that surrounds the Being on the throne. . . . He is a very big God![77]

After dying from a pulmonary embolism, Randy Kay describes the awe and wonder he felt when Jesus ushered him before the throne of God.

> Once I entered into this space it was very different. . . . There was more gravity about this place, . . . a power in this place that caused overwhelming awe. I was struck by the intensity of what was around me. Even the angels I'd seen while in Heaven were different

> around the Throne. They were majestic looking. . . . I looked upon this altar, which was more of a . . . crystalline formation, and there was this "flowing," like there would be frozen water or crystal in the background and all these vivid colors shining forth. . . . I looked to the floor and saw it was blue—cobalt blue, and there were what looked like flames that were emitting from the floor. . . . Then, Jesus pointed to the Throne, and it wasn't like a chair, . . . this was a place where this figure appeared, and he was gargantuan in size. . . . I was a bit bedazzled, but I felt that the Father gave me this tremendous assurance that I was protected. The Father in his might, because he was so awe-inspiring in his appearance, . . . would protect me.[78]

....

The presence of the Father at the throne of God constitutes the most glorious, powerful, and awe-inspiring sense of wonder we could ever imagine. His magnificence causes all creation to drop to their knees in awe, in a reverent "fear" of the Almighty God. Yet there is nothing to be afraid of in his loving arms.

God uses his mighty power to strengthen us when we are weary and support us when we are humble and seek his help. "The Lord is the everlasting God, the Creator of all the earth. He never grows weak or weary. . . . He gives power to the weak and strength to the powerless" (Isaiah 40:28-29). Even when we go through trials and sufferings, we have nothing to fear when we are in the hands of our awesome God.

Whenever you feel exhausted from the battles of life or when your strength is failing, turn to our powerful, amazing God.

Worship him and allow him to strengthen and uplift you, no matter what you are going through. Remember, with God, you can conquer anything! God says, "I will strengthen you and help you. I will hold you up with my victorious right hand" (Isaiah 41:10).

When you turn to God for strength, this is an act of faith that shows him you trust in his goodness and love. Remember, he promises to uphold you with his mighty hand. Where do you need strength to face the challenges ahead? Bring your difficulties before the throne of God today. Keep your eyes fixed on Jesus and draw from God's limitless resources. He is your source of inspiration, hope, and power, and he will provide a way forward for you, no matter what situation you are facing.

PRAYER

Father God, you are awesome in power, Ruler of the universe, and King of my life. I will trust you now with all my worries and fears because you are my protection and my strength. I have nothing to fear when I bring my concerns to you, so I release them to you today. I know I am safe in your mighty hands.

27

Healing Light

"I have seen their ways, but I will heal them; I will guide them and restore comfort to Israel's mourners, creating praise on their lips. Peace, peace, to those far and near," says the LORD. "And I will heal them."

ISAIAH 57:18-19, NIV

In Indonesia, a young man named Ian McCormack died from box jellyfish poisoning but was later revived. As he realized he was dying, he knew he needed to turn to God for forgiveness. He prayed to Jesus, the God his mother had followed all her life. He describes God's glorious light and the healing love and forgiveness that washed over him during his near-death experience.

> I came out of the end of the tunnel and seemed to be standing upright before the source of all the light and power. My whole vision was taken up with this incredible light. It looked like a white fire or a mountain of cut diamonds sparkling with the most indescribable brilliance. I immediately thought of it as aura, then as glory. I had seen pictures of Jesus with a little halo or small glow around his face, yet this glory was all-encompassing, overwhelming, awe-inspiring. . . . As I stepped into the light it was as if I'd come inside veils of suspended shimmering lights, like suspended stars or diamonds giving off the most

> amazing radiance. And as I walked through the light it continued to heal the deepest part of me. . . .
>
> So this was God! He is light. He knew my name and he knew the secret thoughts of my heart and mind. . . . You can wear masks before other people, but you can't wear a mask before God. I felt ashamed and undone and I thought, "I shouldn't be here. I'm not a very good person." As I began to slowly move back towards the tunnel, . . . to my amazement a wave of pure unconditional love flowed over me. It was the last thing I expected. Instead of judgement, I was being washed with pure love. Pure, unadulterated, clean, uninhibited, undeserved, love. . . . God showed me that when I'd asked for forgiveness in the ambulance, it was then that he forgave me and washed my spirit clean from evil. . . . This love was healing my heart, and I began to understand that there is incredible hope for humankind in this love.[79]

Critical care nurse Penny Wittbrodt and her three children had been abandoned by Penny's husband when her children were very young. Penny watched her children experience increasing pain and rejection as, year after year, their father would promise a birthday gift but never send it, promise to call but always forget, or promise to come by but rarely show up. The hurt of watching her children internalize their father's lies—believing there was something wrong with them for their father to reject them so—tore at the fabric of Penny's faith and planted bitterness deep in her heart. Yet when Penny went into anaphylactic shock from an allergic reaction and had an NDE, she finally found healing in God's light and presence.

> So, I'm there with God, talking about the kids, and I needed more healing. I'm in this Light, and this healing process begins where the Light comes through my feet, creeping up through my body, spiritually healing every cell.[80] . . . So he's in me now (the light in me)—and it goes up to my middle. And I had all those feelings of angst and visceral gut feelings that he was healing from within. He's healing those cellular memories of hurt. And the light comes out my tongue and I start singing, and then when it gets to my brain there's a euphoric feeling and I didn't want it to stop.[81]

....

God's light is alive—a powerful and healing force that exudes an indescribable, larger-than-life love, permeating every cell of our being in his presence. Imagine the day when we are in the physical presence of this light of love, feeling the absolute healing we have longed for all of our lives. In God's presence, we will finally become fully and completely whole. No more broken or unhealed pieces of ourselves will remain—pieces that, in our humanity, continue to cause us pain and hold us back from facets of joy and freedom we were designed to experience fully in Christ.

Even in our broken world, as believers, we can be assured that God is still shining his light on us and in us. "For God, who said, 'Let there be light in the darkness,' has made this light shine in our hearts" (2 Corinthians 4:6). In Christ, the darkness and pain inside us can be brought into his light and be healed. God declares, "I am the LORD who heals you" (Exodus 15:26).

Jesus is the light of life that heals us, and he wants us to come to him for restoration and wholeness when we have been hurt. He knows we can't heal ourselves alone.

Imagine feeling the warmth of his light filling every part of your body, mind, and spirit—healing those places you've longed to have restored, replacing dark places with his everlasting light, and bringing them back to life again. Take some time today to meditate on this truth, because God's healing light and love are shining on you now!

PRAYER

Dear God, thank you that in you there is no darkness. Please shine your light of love and mercy upon me and show me what you want to heal in my soul. Help me to receive the powerful healing you desire to give me in every dark or wounded area of my heart as I turn toward you now.

28

God Understands Us

This High Priest of ours understands our weaknesses, for he faced all of the same testings we do, yet he did not sin. So let us come boldly to the throne of our gracious God. There we will receive his mercy, and we will find grace to help us when we need it most.

HEBREWS 4:15-16

What twelve-year-old Susanne Seymoure experienced during a skiing accident was vastly different from what those observing her back on earth saw. While her mother was screaming hysterically and her grandparents were in shock, Susanne encountered Jesus and experienced inexplicable joy and peace far greater than she could ever have imagined!

> What I remember just before I hit the gearbox is finding myself lying in the snow, and on the side of me I'm seeing birch trees and pine trees, because I'm drawn to a human figure in a white robe and light all around him. At first, I thought it was my dad. There were two others behind him I thought might be my mom and grandmother. I thought it was my dad because he felt so loving. And I just knew he was going to help me, and rescue me, and come and get me. I felt there was a sense of urgency. As soon as he came close, he put his hands out and looked at me, and through

his eyes he just tells you exactly who he is. "I'm Jesus." And I just felt all this love and light, and I'm thinking, *I don't really know Jesus,* but he felt so loving. And next to him were these two angels, but I didn't know to call them angels.[82]

There was a calm and a comfort that is hard to find the words for.[83] . . . It's as if every cell in my body, every need, every concern, every emotion, everything about me and my life is heard and understood in a matter of a moment, . . . my protections and barriers peeled away.[84] . . . I felt no fear; he was like the most loving parent multiplied by a thousand. The hardest thing is to find the words for something that is so amazing. It was so remarkable that to this day there has not been a single experience that could ever compare.[85] . . .

The light was his light. The light immediately came around me, and then my focus was on Jesus and his hands. He put out his hands, and all this information was conveyed: "Everything is going to be all right." If you've never met Jesus, he tells you everything about himself in an instant. There's no question. And it's like he lets your whole body know [that] he knows everything about you. Everything. Just feeling that understood—my mind, my heart, everything felt so understood. It felt like he knew my whole life in a second. So, there was no fear because we had this instant "I've known you all my life" connection.

He picked me up, scooped me in his arms. He was holding me, and the angels were shielding me on either side. And I was in a state of joy—home, bliss, happy. There's just so much joy. I never felt more loved or more joyful—and happy, euphorically happy.[86]

. . . .

With Jesus, we are completely understood, fully known, and unconditionally loved. And in the security of being so understood, there will be joy and bliss indescribable in his presence!

The writer of Hebrews reminds us that God understands our weaknesses, insecurities, and all we go through in life because Jesus went through it all himself. And Jesus, as our great High Priest, offered the perfect sacrifice with his own blood, so we can have access directly to God's throne. We can come boldly to God and receive mercy and help for whatever we need.

Knowing that God understands us can set us free when we feel misunderstood or unfairly judged by others. So many times, people will not understand our hearts or motives. Our actions may be taken the wrong way, and our good intentions may backfire. Jesus himself was misunderstood, misrepresented, and even mischaracterized as evil. But as Scripture reminds us, "Our purpose is to please God, not people. He alone examines the motives of our hearts" (1 Thessalonians 2:4). What great freedom there is in knowing that God—the only one whose opinion really matters—always understands us perfectly and loves us completely!

Imagine feeling wholly known and perfectly understood, with no fears or insecurities holding you back. You are fully understood by God, *right now*. As Scripture says, there is "one God and Father of all, who is over all, in all, and living through all" (Ephesians 4:6).

Take a moment and think about the amazing truth that God has always been with you and always will be. He perfectly understands every thought, desire, and motive, including the times when you've felt misunderstood or alone. He has been with you every second of your life—through every high and low—and he's *still* with you. Today, let the comfort of being fully known and loved fill your heart with his joyful gladness, reassuring you that you are secure in him forever.

PRAYER

Dear God, thank you for understanding me perfectly. No one else has been with me through it all. You understand all I've gone through, all that's shaped me, every motive; and you love me with immeasurable love. Help me live to please you, not people, so I can live in the security and understanding only you can give.

29

Our Perfect Guide

When the Spirit of truth comes, he will guide you into all truth. He will not speak on his own but will tell you what he has heard. He will tell you about the future. He will bring me glory by telling you whatever he receives from me.

JOHN 16:13-14

God promises to guide us through life by his Holy Spirit and to always be with us. However, the way his perfect guidance works often feels mysterious. At times, it may not feel like he is guiding us at all. Yet those who have had near-death experiences have come to the realization that God's guidance is always present and available to all who seek it.

When Jim Woodford died of an accidental opioid overdose, he cried out to God for forgiveness. During his NDE, as Jim walked and talked with his guardian angel, he saw six streaks of light streaming across the sky like shooting stars. The Guardian told Jim that those were the prayers of his loved ones for him at that very moment. Then the angel explained how important it is to God for us to talk to him and seek his guidance.

> He saw the tears in my eyes, from my family praying for me. And he said, "James, sadly, mankind is losing the will to pray." He said, "Your forefathers, when they would finish their day's work in the fields or the factories, after dinner, they had what used to be

called Eventide. And they would read the Bible and pray as a family." And he said, "Sadly, they are losing that. And with all your technology of instantaneous gratification—you can call anywhere in the world and speak face-to-face with someone, and that is a wonderful achievement of the intelligence that God gave you. But sadly, now, when mankind gets a few spare minutes at the end of a busy day, they check Facebook, text, Instagram. And there's nothing wrong with that, but remember this, when you have those rare moments of peace in a busy life, that's God giving you a little time, and he wants you to sit and talk to him. Listen for the sound of God's voice, and hear him say to you, 'Be at peace my son, my daughter. I am with you always.'"

The angel said, "Every prayer you've ever issued, every thought ever contemplated, is recorded in Heaven.[87] . . . Your prayers are recorded to show you during your life review all the things that you prayed for that didn't happen. God will one day show you, when a prayer was not answered, it was because God knew it would not be good for you. And yet, you can power through with your own free will to try and make it happen." The Guardian explained to me that God has absolute respect for our free will because love can never be taken, it can only be given. He will not violate our free will because free will is necessary for love.[88]

Randy Kay, who died of a pulmonary embolism, shares that during his near-death experience, he walked with Jesus in heaven. On his walk, he gained valuable insight into how God's guidance is ever present and constant—we only need to listen.

> Jesus was saying things audibly. Initially I thought that he was speaking to me, both without words, and speaking to me audibly. And because Jesus and the Holy Spirit were One, I came to realize through this understanding, this revelation, that he was speaking to me both ways, audibly and without words. But the times that I heard him without words, in understanding, that was the Holy Spirit.[89] . . . I learned a valuable lesson from Heaven, and that is the Holy Spirit is speaking to us constantly, and we're just not listening. When Paul talked about praying unceasingly, I would always think, *How can you do that? The cares of the world—we can't be ever-presently minded*. . . . I realized as I walked with Jesus, he knew those cares, he had compassion for how we go through the struggles in this life. . . . I knew I could go to him 24-7, and even when I was sleeping, he'd be there. So, now my prayers are in conversation, . . . going to the grocery store, and just saying, "Lord, what am I supposed to be doing here?" Somebody's over there, and I hear the Holy Spirit speaking, "This person over here needs some prayer."[90]

....

When we put our faith in Jesus, God has promised his Holy Spirit will always be with us, guiding us toward our life's purpose. From the beginning of time, God has always guided his children. As Exodus 15:13 says, "With your unfailing love you lead the people you have redeemed. In your might, you guide them." And guidance involves hearing from him.

We are meant to be in ongoing conversation with God—the one who knows us best, loves us most, and is always with us to lead us. God respects the free will he gave us, so he works within our prayer lives to guide us without overriding our will, even when we make choices that aren't the best for us. If we get off track by not listening to his guidance, he will lead us back once we turn to him. God never gives up on us.

God wants to do life with us! We can talk to him about everything—nothing is too big or too small to bring to him. As we listen and discern, God leads us through the Holy Spirit's promptings, helping us to make the right decisions toward the purpose and plan God created uniquely for each of us. The Holy Spirit speaks to our minds constantly, but we must learn to listen.

Jesus said, "Anyone with ears to hear must listen to the Spirit" (Revelation 2:7). We develop spiritual "ears to hear" as we moment-by-moment seek the Holy Spirit's guidance and obey his promptings. Begin taking time to listen for any nudges that the Holy Spirit may be giving you, and take a step to respond in faith. The more you step out to follow his promptings in obedience, the more confident you will feel about clearly discerning his thoughts from your own, and this takes practice.

Remember, try not to rush ahead of God—let him be your leader. He will give you next steps of faith to take, moment by moment. And be encouraged, knowing that God is guiding you in his perfect plan for your life. As you converse with him throughout the day, stay willing to do the next right thing. That's all you need to do. Remember the words of Jesus: "My purpose is to give them a rich and satisfying life" (John 10:10). Today, stay in step with his Spirit and find hope in the purpose-filled future that he promises you.

PRAYER

Lord, thank you for the promise that once I have put my faith in you, your Holy Spirit is always with me, speaking to me and guiding me. Help me, today, to remain in conversation with you, willing to do your will, so that you can lead me to become all I am meant to be.

30

Unfailing Mercy and Compassion

But you, O Lord, are a God of compassion and mercy, slow to get angry and filled with unfailing love and faithfulness.

PSALM 86:15

In London, England, Mary sped to the hospital by ambulance, bleeding severely with complications due to pregnancy. As soon as she arrived at the emergency room, the staff came running into the room. She was in a life-threatening, extremely critical condition. Mary recalls what happened next.

> I heard a "pop" sound and suddenly the pain stopped. I felt calm for the first time in three months since learning of my pregnancy by a man who had lied to me, telling me he loved me and wanted to marry me, but who had a wife and five children in another city. I had a very clear view of my body as they ferociously worked on me, hooking up a transfusion and other tubes. I recalled thinking that I just wished they would stop. . . . I had sinned and didn't deserve to live. . . . I was aware of a tunnel that appeared suddenly. . . . [I] was overwhelmed by a radiant white light that seemed to embody all the concepts of love. A love that was unconditional and like a mother has for a child. It was definitely a warm

> joyful presence . . . that radiated all the good and noble emotions known to man. I had given up the ways of the Catholic church, . . . but I knew in my heart that this was God. Words can't describe my awe in this presence.[91]

During this time, God showed Mary her life. She said he knew her every thought and feeling, and she never wanted to leave his presence. As he gave her a life review, Mary not only observed each moment, but she experienced her life all over again, including the impact of every good or bad action. Yet through it all, she felt his compassion and loving support, even while reviewing the scenes she regretted.

> It was a difficult time for me, but I was supported by [God's] unconditional love and weathered the painful parts. I was asked telepathically about whether I wanted to stay or return. . . . I fell to my knees in order to show my desire to stay with Him.[92]

After her life review, God told Mary that her baby would live, and he would send her back to be there for him. No matter what hardship she'd been through—from choices made by others or her own choices—the love of God broke through it all. Even though she had turned away from God as far as she understood, God had never turned away from her. His loving-kindness and compassionate forgiveness enveloped her heart, and she knew for certain that he was *for* her. In the presence of God, Mary felt washed clean, forgiven, and unconditionally loved.

. . . .

God's compassionate love for you is unlike anything earthly words can describe. No matter what you've done, or what circumstances have fallen upon you by other people, God's loving compassion for you never runs out. And it's not dependent on anything you do or don't do for him. He loves you unconditionally and completely, no matter what! Romans 8:38-39 says,

> I am convinced that nothing can ever separate us from God's love. Neither death nor life, neither angels nor demons, neither our fears for today nor our worries about tomorrow—not even the powers of hell can separate us from God's love. No power in the sky above or in the earth below—indeed, nothing in all creation will ever be able to separate us from the love of God that is revealed in Christ Jesus our Lord.

As you grow to fully embrace God's limitless mercy and love, you will naturally be filled with the desire to become more like him, showing the same compassionate love toward others that he generously bestows upon you. Take some time now to meditate on the magnitude of God's infinite love and compassion for you. Allow his heart to come close to yours, no matter how far you may feel from him. Remember, he loves you more than you could ever imagine, and he longs to draw near to you now.

PRAYER

Dear God, no matter what I've done or what others have done to me, your loving compassion and forgiveness is bigger than it all. Thank you for your unconditional love for me. Help me to let it comfort and flood my heart today, so that I can be a conduit of your mercy and compassion to others.

31

King of Kings

I saw the Lord, high and exalted, seated on a throne; and the train of his robe filled the temple.

ISAIAH 6:1, NIV

Captain Dale Black, a commercial airline pilot, miraculously came back from death after a twin-engine plane crash took the lives of everyone except him. During his near-death experience, God gave him a flyover of the majestic city of God where God's throne was the magnificent focal point:

> I got this descending, airborne view of the City of God. It's a city. It's a city that's walled. . . . Over the city were majestic mountains that were as gorgeous as any that could ever be seen. . . . The wall was gigantic. It looked like it was a couple hundred feet high. It was made of very dense stone, yet it was translucent. You could see through it. The light from the throne room of God was permeating through the stones, giving life to everything. . . . The light which came from the city center was holy and thick and pure. . . . There was a stairway that was near a glass sea, which did look like a sea; and a stairway that went up [to the throne]. . . . I was beginning to recognize that I'm being infused with power, like there's some nuclear power plant on the

inside of me, but the power is coming from the light, and that light is giving energy.[93]

The magnificent light I was experiencing emanated from about forty or fifty miles within the city wall. I saw a great phosphorescent display of light that narrowed to a focal point that was brighter than the sun. Oddly, it didn't make me squint to look at it. And all I wanted to do was to look at it. The light was palpable. It had substance to it, weight and thickness, like nothing I had ever seen before or since. The light from a hydrogen bomb is the closest I can come to describing it.[94]

Dean Braxton, who died of sepsis, recalls that God's throne is not a typical king's throne, but just as Ezekiel reported, it is more like a cloud that goes with him (see Ezekiel 1:4).

The throne is not like we picture; it looked more like a cloud than a chair. Like [the cloud] at the Transfiguration of Jesus or at Mount Sinai,[95] the throne goes with him—it's part of him. It's not a room or building; it seemed to be more open. The Father was on his throne, but it was open, like all of heaven, not one little place.[96]

When Gregg Rickert had a near-death experience after being hit head-on in an automobile collision, he saw God's throne and the angels Isaiah described in Isaiah 6:1-3.

I find myself in the throne room of God. I look up, and I see angels kneeling down with their arms over their faces from the glory of God—you know where you are! I see this glowing, bright white, unexplainably powerful light shining from his face. The music is coming from

> all over, even vibrating from the essence of my being—the body I am in—and from the walls and floors of heaven itself. It is the most beautiful, indescribable, perfect feeling of joy and peace that one could ever experience—something we are designed for and something we cannot experience in this earthly reality. The music is joy and worship of God, and all of it is going to God in the throne room. The angels are twelve to fifteen feet tall. God is much bigger than a man. I am not thinking about how big he is, just how wonderful. There are angels all around him in complete reverence, and they have wings over their faces. God is sitting in a white robe—a blinding light of perfection. There's no doubt this is God. There's no question who this is or where you are—this is God the Father and his throne. I might have been there a long time, but it never gets old. Every fiber of my being is bursting with joy.[97]

....

"Blessed are you O Lord, our God, King of the universe." This is how traditional Jewish prayers often began, acknowledging God first as King of all. A kingdom is any place where the rule and reign, or the will and ways, of the king are accomplished. God, the King of kings, reigns forever, and his Kingdom will never end.

In heaven, many people who have had NDEs see glimpses of God the Father on his throne, a king who rules over the Kingdom of Heaven. They confirm that heaven is the most harmonious, peaceful, loving, and joyful place for its inhabitants, because all creatures gladly follow the King's will and ways.

In contrast, here on earth, we are constantly faced with the challenge of allowing God to rule our lives. It is a battle of wills as each of us struggles to submit to our King's authority. When we choose to go against God's will and try to control our lives on our own, we are basically "playing God" and deciding, "I know what's best for my own life—*my* will be done." Consider how much time we spend each day thinking about our own desires and plans versus seeking God's will for our lives. We must learn to ask, "What do you want me to do today, Lord? What is your will for this situation?"

This is exactly why Jesus taught us to pray, "Our Father, . . . *your* kingdom come, *your* will be done, on earth as it is in heaven" (Matthew 6:9-10, NIV, emphasis added). God's Kingdom comes to earth through us together, as we each voluntarily submit our wills to the will of God. Are you recognizing God as the rightful King and Ruler of your life, and are you trusting him as the King of kings?

It is reassuring to know that one day, Jesus will return as King, and he will unite heaven and earth under his leadership forever. As it says in Revelation 11:15, "The kingdom of the world has become the kingdom of our Lord and of his Messiah, and he will reign for ever and ever" (NIV). Today, take some time to think about where you may find yourself trying to control things that are not yours to rule, and then graciously give that authority back to God. When you do this, you will find that the love, peace, and genuine joy of heaven will be yours, today as well as forever.

PRAYER

Blessed are you, O Lord, our God, King of the universe. I acknowledge you as my King, and I want to let your will and your ways have leadership over my little kingdom today. May your Kingdom come as I let your will be done in my life each moment.

32

Unconditional Acceptance

Therefore, accept each other just as Christ has accepted you so that God will be given glory.

ROMANS 15:7

It was not guilt but love that led Cedric Pisegna into the priesthood. Yet he knew very well the shame and regret that come with a life of self-centeredness and egocentric desires. At age twenty, he was drowning in guilt. He knew he had separated himself from connection to God due to all the bad choices he'd made. He prayed that God would forgive him—and had no idea he would experience an encounter with God shortly thereafter during his near-death experience.

The forgiveness, love, and acceptance he felt from God overwhelmed him.

> As I stood close to the Glorious person of God, I had an awakening to the Holy Spirit at the Throne of God, and I knew it was Jesus who took me to the Throne. . . . Jesus had his arm around my neck. . . . The fact that he would put his arm around a twenty-year-old who had had an abortion, and that he would treat me like an intimate friend, melted my heart. [But] he's a friend of the outcast, the marginalized,

the poor. It was [due to] Jesus, because of his passion, that I was summoned to the Throne of God, because of my humble seeking prayer. I sensed Jesus' radiant smile. I was beaming, and Jesus was radiant. He taught about the joy in heaven when someone lost is found, and I can tell you from experience, there is ethereal jubilation![98]

As I stood before God, I experienced a life review. . . . In a flash, my life was simply laid bare. There was no hiding, no pretending, and no putting on. There were no excuses to make. . . . I drank, smoked marijuana, dated and partied with girls. I didn't pray or attend Mass and didn't give to anyone but myself. . . . My life revolved around me. I was very selfish, narcissistic, and stingy. Sad to say, I used people and loved things to find happiness. . . .

As I stood before Love itself, I realized to my shame that I wasn't even close to being a loving person. The opposite of love is not hate. The opposite of love is selfishness. Love is generous and cares. Selfishness is stingy and cares only for itself. . . . Through his grace, I was forgiven and declared upright before him by the blood of Jesus. . . .

When I encountered God's love, I came to know in the depths of my being that God had been for me, not against me! Throughout my life, I haven't been able to manage my behavior as I want. In spite of my powerlessness, I have found that God actually helps me rather than condemns me. . . . If I stumble along the way, it is God himself who picks me up. If I fail, it is God who forgives me. When I am weak, it is God who gives me strength. "If God is for us, who can be

> against us?" (Romans 8:31). As I left God's presence, I promised: "Now that I know, I will be my best!"[99]

Cedric knew that God wanted his actions to change, but the overwhelming acceptance and intimate love from God is what eventually led Cedric to become a priest and begin helping others understand God's grace and acceptance offered through the cross of Christ.

After delivering her second child, Alexa Hartung looked down and saw she was bleeding profusely. As the doctors scrambled to save her, she left her body. Alexa also found herself before God's throne, watching her life review.

> I fell on my face in shame. I saw how my acting, or not acting, rippled in effect toward other people and their lives. It wasn't until then that I understood how each little decision or choice affects the World. The sense of letting my Savior down was too real. Strangely, even during this horror, I felt a compassion, an acceptance of my limitations by Jesus.[100]

....

God is a loving Father who accepts us unconditionally—*as is*. Perhaps at some point in life we felt we had to jump through certain hoops or hit certain marks in order to be accepted and loved. Some of us may have experienced feelings of rejection from peer groups, organizations, churches, or even our own families when we didn't measure up to certain standards, spoken or unspoken. This is never the case with God! He created you and believes the best in you. Jesus paid an enormous price for you. Nothing you have ever done nor could ever do can change how God feels about you. He knows your potential and has a purpose for your life, one that only you can fulfill.

Remember, no matter what temptations and trials come against you, God is on your team and fights for you and for your good, as Romans 8:31 assures. He won't force his will and ways, but he is always *for* you—the "you" he created—and he is ready at all times to help you be the best version of yourself you can be. Knowing that God is walking with you, picking you up when you fall, strengthening you when you're weak, and encouraging you when you fail can motivate you to give him your best—out of gratitude and a full heart. He delights in you, his child! He accepts you as you are and wants to help you become all he intends for you to be. Meditate on this truth today: God is *for* me!

PRAYER

Dear God, thank you for accepting me and loving me just as I am. Knowing you are for me, not against me, gives me courage to trust you to help me become the best version of myself I can be.

33

I Am

God replied to Moses, "I Am Who I Am. Say this to the people of Israel: I Am has sent me to you." God also said to Moses, "Say this to the people of Israel: Yahweh, the God of your ancestors—the God of Abraham, the God of Isaac, and the God of Jacob—has sent me to you. This is my eternal name, my name to remember for all generations."

EXODUS 3:14-15

Bibi Tahereh speaks only Persian and is related to the prophet Muhammad. She helped build a mosque in her Tehran neighborhood, an esteemed gated community, where she lived next door to a prominent government official. When her two adult children became followers of Jesus, Bibi was so distraught with heart-crushing guilt and anxiety, it literally killed her as she lay in bed one night. Bibi explained,

> That night I was so hopeless, feeling I was not a good servant to Allah, that I had failed, and my children had gone astray. The pain was so great that sometime in the night, I had a heart attack. My heart stopped. I saw my spirit leave my body, and I found myself in another world.[101]

Bibi knew she was dead and fearfully waited for the Imam Ali to come to judge her, as Shiite Muslims believe happens after death. She saw a vision of her burial and a large stone hitting her head, which in Shiite tradition meant she would be condemned as a horrible sinner. She waited in fear, but Imam Ali didn't come.

Instead, Bibi saw a giant man in a majestic white robe approach her.

> He was so tall and his robe very long. I was trembling and shaking. There was a presence of power and strength about him, and I could look at his face, but I didn't recognize the face at the time.[102]

The man spoke thought-to-thought to Bibi and said in Persian, "I AM HE WHO IS."

> When the man said, "I AM HE WHO IS," my soul fell back into my body, and I woke up alive again, but with a peace I had never experienced before.[103] . . . What just happened to me? I had been expecting a harsh judgment, as I knew I was a terrible sinner, but now I felt an overwhelming peace after hearing the Man say "I AM."

She lay there feeling great peace in her heart, more than she'd ever felt in her life. It covered all the hurt, shame, and bad feelings. "At that time," Bibi recalls, "I didn't know what 'I AM' meant because I didn't know anything about the Bible or Jesus."

After this divine encounter in her near-death experience, Bibi felt an immense new joy and freedom. Inside, she desperately wanted to know who this God was, the one who loved her so much and called himself "I AM." So Bibi spent the next year praying, seeking, and asking God to reveal himself to her. And that next New Year's Eve, as her adult children prayed for her, Bibi had a vision.

> I again could see the man in the white robe. The first time [in the NDE], he looked huge, with a white robe [and] without a discernible face. The second time, he was our size and had a human face, like a glorious king with a scepter in his hands. I grabbed his robe, and he was so close I could touch his face. The second I touched his face, I knew this was Jesus. Jesus was the face of the unknown God.[104]

....

While on earth, Jesus spoke of the mystery of his eternal nature. He told the Pharisees who were plotting to kill him, "Your father Abraham rejoiced as he looked forward to my coming," to which they sneered, "You aren't even fifty years old. How can you say you have seen Abraham?" Jesus then replied, "I tell you the truth, before Abraham was even born, I Am!" (see John 8:56-58).

"I Am!" Jesus equated himself with Yahweh, the God who appeared to Moses in a burning bush in the desert near Mount Sinai, declaring his eternal nature, "I Am Who I Am" (Exodus 3:14). Jesus clearly declared himself God who is eternal: "I am the one who is, who always was, and who is still to come—the Almighty One. . . . I am the First and the Last. I am the living one. I died, but look—I am alive forever and ever!" (Revelation 1:8, 17-18).

Because God is eternal, his perspective of time is complete. He experiences your creation, every moment of your life, and even the wonderful resolution of all your trials and tribulations all at once in his eternal joy. As humans, we change with time and our circumstances change with time; yet God *never* changes—he is, he was, and he will forever be the eternal I Am.

God is constant through all the uncertainties our experience of time brings. We can count on God's everlasting love and depend on him as our never-failing rock, our fortress, our safe harbor in the storms of life. Because he sees past, present, and future simultaneously, he can be trusted to forever love us and guide us from here into eternity. There's so much comfort and security in following the great "I Am!"

Are you facing changes or challenges that leave you feeling overwhelmed with fear, like there is no solution ahead? You can trust in God, the great I Am. He already sees the solution to your concerns and will guide you as you look to him. Perhaps you may be anxious about the future or worried about your health, kids, marriage, or work relationships. God's eternal nature can bring you peace today! He can be trusted and cares about everything you care about, so give all your anxiety to him and walk confidently forward in the blessings he has planned for you.

Remember, God already knows the victory that will come, and he will be faithful to lead you there. Today, right now, surrender your fears and worries into God's care and rest in the assurance that he promises to be with you and guide you every step of the way—from here to eternity!

PRAYER

Yahweh, the great "I Am," thank you for revealing yourself through Jesus. Sometimes I forget just how great you are, and I try to control the future rather than trusting the one who is already working in my best future. Today I put the past and future in your hands, and I will follow you in each present moment, knowing you have wonderful things planned for me.

34

Positive Minded

No one can know a person's thoughts except that person's own spirit, and no one can know God's thoughts except God's own Spirit. And we have received God's Spirit (not the world's spirit), so we can know the wonderful things God has freely given us. . . . We understand these things, for we have the mind of Christ.

1 CORINTHIANS 2:11-12, 16

Penny Wittbrodt's husband abandoned her and their kids, which left her with hurts and resentments she struggled with for years. During her near-death experience after an allergic reaction caused her heart to stop, God gave Penny a very enlightening life review. After he showed her all the good things she had done, he revealed the power of her negative thoughts about others and how replacing them with positive thoughts is crucial to mirror God's mindset.

> Then we went through some of the negative things, and the one thing that really stuck with me was that, of all the things I've done in my life that I'm not proud of, the thing shown to me is probably the hardest thing to never do again. And it was to control my thoughts about other people.
>
> God showed me the negative thoughts I carried, and He said, "Let me explain something to you. A

thought has a certain energy to it. A word has even more. And an action has even more than that. But it all starts with a thought."

There's something in the Bible that says, the mouth is like the rudder of the ship. The way you speak is the direction you go. And there's life and death in the tongue. Well, it's the same thing with your thoughts. What you think about is what you talk about is what you end up doing. It starts in the mind.

He showed me these negative thoughts I had about people, and they were deserved, let me tell you! These were some really jerky people. But He said, "When you spend your energy on this and you're thinking these negative thoughts, it hurts you, because the energy impacts you."

Then He showed me how my negative thoughts about them [are] like energy that attaches to them and only increases their tendency to be that way. And this is why forgiving is so important. . . . When I forgive you, that energy is able to be redirected. So it's really important to that other person's journey for you to forgive them, and it's really important to you because that negative energy attaches to you.[105]

....

First Corinthians 2:16 says that believers have been given the mind of Christ, so we must surrender our minds to his ways of thinking. When we fill our minds with God's thoughts about ourselves and others, we sow God's goodness and reflect his love. God's mindset toward people is always one of hope and a positive future. Ephesians 2:10 tells us that when God looks at people, he sees the masterpiece he created each person to be. That masterpiece may be stained and torn, yet his grace can restore it fully. God sees in his mind's eye the potential a person can reach, even when they are far from it. "While we were still sinners, Christ died for us" (Romans 5:8, NIV).

God sees hope and positive potential in every person because he knows he's already won every battle and will redeem all suffering and pain, heal every wound, and restore every broken relationship for all those who follow him. This is the mindset of Christ we must adopt toward other people, and it has the power to make a significant impact.

Human nature lends itself to complaining, grumbling, and negative thinking about situations and others. That's why, in the Sermon on the Mount, Jesus strongly urges his followers to let that go. The consequences of projecting those negative attitudes and actions will only end up heading straight back to us. Jesus said, "Do not judge others, and *you will not be judged.* Do not condemn others, *or it will all come back against you.* Forgive others, *and you will be forgiven*" (Luke 6:37, emphasis added). In the same way, forgiving and letting go of negative thoughts and embracing a positive mindset toward ourselves and others, creates positive, forward momentum that can move us and others in God's direction.

The apostle Paul says, "Fix your thoughts on what is true, and honorable, and right, and pure, and lovely, and admirable. Think about things that are excellent and worthy of praise" (Philippians 4:8). As we do this, we align our minds with the mind of Christ. To *fix* our thoughts doesn't just mean to temporarily change them—it means "to make firm, stable," "to give a permanent or final form to."[106] This is not easy. We must throw out the negative thoughts and firmly replace them with thoughts that are praiseworthy, honorable, and lovely.

Today, ask God to help you form a new habit of being permeated with positive, life-giving thoughts instead of negative ones. Think of ways you can project hope and possibilities in your attitude toward others and clean out any thoughts of the contrary. You will love the results! When you fix your thoughts on the mind of Christ, you will increase your joy, notice the goodness of God all around you, call out positive potential in people, and make a greater impact in the world.

PRAYER

Dear God, thank you for giving me the mind of Christ. Help me to fix my thoughts on things that are honorable and praiseworthy and not dwell on critical, negative thinking about others or situations. I want to have your mindset that sees the good potential in everything and everyone, including myself, to make a positive difference in the world.

35

Eternal Joy

I have told you these things so that you will be filled with my joy.
Yes, your joy will overflow!

JOHN 15:11

In the year 1898, long before near-death experiences were widely known, Rebecca Springer fell gravely ill from pneumonia and felt herself dying. Next thing she knew, she was standing by her bed, looking at her lifeless body, when her previously deceased brother-in-law, Frank, came and took her to a place of joyful wonders. Rebecca was reunited with her niece, Mae, who had died at a young age, and together they experienced many joys of God's world:

> Away, away—far beyond the limit of my vision, I well knew—stretched this wonderful sward of perfect grass. . . . Not a single blade was any color but the brightest green. The air was soft and balmy, though invigorating; and instead of sunlight there was a golden and rosy glory everywhere. . . . And out of [the grass] grew equally wonderful trees, whose drooping branches were laden with exquisite blossoms and fruits of many kinds. . . .

> Beneath the trees, in many happy groups, were little children, laughing and playing, running hither and thither in their joy, and catching in their tiny hands the bright-winged birds that flitted in and out among them, as though sharing in their sports, as they doubtless were. All through the grounds, older people were walking, sometimes in groups, sometimes by twos, sometimes alone, but all with an air of peacefulness and happiness.[107] . . .
>
> Before us spread a lake as smooth as glass. . . . Many people were resting upon its flowery banks, and on the surface of the water were boats of wonderful structure, filled with happy souls, and propelled by an unseen power. Little children, as well as grown persons, were floating upon or swimming in the water. . . . [Mae] led me into the water, down, down into its crystal depths, and when it seemed to me we must be hundreds of feet beneath the surface, . . . then appeared to me a marvel. Look where I would, perfect prismatic rays surrounded me. I seemed to be resting in the heart of a prism; and such vivid yet delicate coloring, mortal eyes never rested upon. . . . As I lay watching this marvelous panorama, for the colors deepened and faded like the lights of the aurora borealis, I was attracted by the sound of distant music.[108]

Rebecca recognized the tune of the music. Several times she had been delightfully surprised to hear songs she knew and loved on earth. After she and Mae came out of the water, they stood happily watching as children "climbed the trees that overhung the water, with the agility of squirrels, and dropped with happy shouts of laughter into the lake." Rebecca realized what misconceptions we have of God's life. God is the source of all joy, and he gives us life to enjoy!

> Not far from our [heavenly] home we saw a group of children playing upon the grass, and in their midst was a beautiful great dog, over which they were rolling and tumbling with the greatest freedom. As we approached he broke away from them and came bounding to meet us. . . . "Do you not know him, Auntie?" Mae asked brightly. "It is dear old Sport!" I cried, stooping and placing my arms about his neck. . . . "Dear old fellow! How happy I am to have you here!" . . . "He understands every word we say," said Mae. "Of course he does; he only lacks speech to make him perfect. I somehow hoped he might find it here." "He would not be half so interesting if he could talk," said Mae.[109]

Soaking it all in, Rebecca reflected on what Frank told her about heaven:

> One of the delights of this rare life is that no occasion is ever overlooked for reproducing here the pure enjoyments of our mortal life. It is the Father's pleasure to make us realize that this existence is but a continuance of the former life, only without its imperfections and its cares.[110]

Rebecca later reflected after being with Jesus in her NDE that, compared to earth's joys,

> There is a depth, a mystery to all that pertains to the divine life, which I dare not try to describe. . . . Suffice

> it to say, that no joy we know on earth, however rare, however sacred, can be more than the faintest shadow of the joy we there find.[111]

....

C. S. Lewis once said, "Joy is the serious business of heaven."[112] God is the God of joy! He is the source of all joy we've ever experienced in this life or will ever enjoy in the life to come. God is the most joy-filled Being in the universe, and he wants his joy to be our strength and hope as we go through the challenges our lives bring.

The Lord commanded Israel to hold sacred times marked on the calendar for joyous celebration together. They were to acknowledge the God of joy among them because that gives strength in life: "Go and celebrate with a feast of rich foods and sweet drinks, and share gifts of food with people who have nothing prepared. This is a sacred day before our Lord. Don't be dejected and sad, for the joy of the LORD is your strength!" (Nehemiah 8:10).

We gain strength for living when we allow God's joy to infuse all we do. Jesus said, "I am the vine; you are the branches. Those who remain in me, and I in them, will produce much fruit. . . . I have told you these things so that you will be filled with my joy. Yes, your joy will overflow!" (John 15:5, 11). God's joy is given as a birthright to his children. God created you to live with his joy increasing in you and flowing through you. And this joy is not dependent on your circumstances. Even when hard times come, the joy of the Lord will be your strength!

Just like a branch must stay connected to a tree to produce fruit, divine joy comes from staying connected to God, no matter your situation. Find comfort in knowing that true and lasting joy is not dependent on what the world throws your way, which is beyond your control. Instead, genuine, divine joy comes from staying connected to the source of unending joy and happiness—and that true source is God, who never changes. Take some time to meditate on this truth today and experience the eternal joy God desires to give you.

PRAYER

Dear God, everything I've ever loved about this life and all my joy and enjoyment flow from you. I am so grateful. Help me stay connected to you more and more so that I also experience your joy as my strength during hard times, for yours is a joy that no circumstance can take away.

36

All-Knowing Wisdom

All that I know now is partial and incomplete, but then I will know everything completely, just as God now knows me completely.

1 CORINTHIANS 13:12

God has complete knowledge, understanding, and insight into everything that has ever existed or that will exist in the future. Dr. Ron Smothermon, who experienced what he describes as a "bomb blast" of God's qualities during his near-death experience, wrote, "I could feel the presence of His KNOWLEDGE. I had an image of a universe made of libraries, and He wrote every book."[113]

College professor Dr. Colin Perry had insight into the vast understanding of God's knowledge during his NDE. After having a severe heart attack in his garden, Colin coded in the ambulance. He found himself with Jesus and was given a new understanding of who Jesus is.

> I got a real direct line into his awareness. I didn't truly understand who Jesus was until this moment. Jesus was not limited by time. He was aware of all the things in the universe that were happening. I understood that he was seeing through time, through space; he was seeing through all those dimensions infinitely. I could

> have been aware of a bug on a rock. I could have been aware of the dust on the moon. He had an awareness of the whole universe going on—as if he was just connected to all things, and I just felt for a few seconds probably, the immensity of who he is and what sort of power he has. And what sort of love underlies all that power. It was overwhelming, it was magnificent, so beautiful—nothing has compared since, and I won't really be happy until I'm back in his presence. And that is something I will never forget, [something] that explained to me all those words like *omniscient* and *omnipotent* and *sovereign*—all those big words we use to describe God, but to actually feel some small aspect of it was an amazing thing.[114]

....

God fully comprehends every detail of everything and everyone all at once. God also knows all possibilities and how all things will work out in the end. And although this knowledge is too vast and profound for us to adequately comprehend, its reality can help us trust God more when we don't understand what's going on around us. He knows all we've been through, but even more than that, he knows why we've had every thought and understands the motives of our hearts and the reasons we act the way we do. Even when our thoughts or actions do not align with his will, God still has endless compassion for us and never wants us to be afraid to acknowledge our mistakes and shortcomings before him. As we surrender to him, God's unconditional love works with his limitless knowledge, transforming us into the people he created us to be. As King David declared in Psalm 139:1, 6, "O Lord, you have examined my heart and know everything about me. . . . Such knowledge is too wonderful for me, too great for me to understand!"

God wants us to trust him and walk with him through life, gleaning from his perfect wisdom and knowledge as he guides and mentors us. That's how we grow into the best versions of ourselves! It's reassuring to think about how God knows all things, even how every little aspect of every person's life affects the other for humanity's ultimate good. This can bring greater trust in God, especially when we don't understand why things may be unfolding as they are in the present. He oversees and understands how the free-willed choices of billions of people, both good and bad, can be worked together for our good as we follow him. We can lean into his understanding, and not our own, for our security, and that is liberating! We can trust the wisdom of Solomon in Proverbs 3:5-6: "Trust in the Lord with all your heart and lean not on your own understanding; in all your ways submit to him, and he will make your paths straight" (NIV).

Today, take some time to reflect on areas of your life that you find hard to surrender to God. He wants you to trust him as the all-knowing one who loves you and wants the very best for you. You can be free of anxiety, fear, and worry over things you don't understand because you follow the one who understands it all! And remember, Philippians 1:6 promises that "he who began a good work in you will carry it on to completion until the day of Christ Jesus" (NIV). You are safe with God, and he will always work things out for your good as you give control of your life back to him.

PRAYER

O Lord, your thoughts and understanding are so beyond me. Forgive me for when I've acted like I know best. I want to trust your infinite knowledge and wisdom. Please show me what you see in my heart, and help me trust your understanding, not my own. Thank you for working all things for my good in your infinite wisdom and love.

37

Jesus, Our Mediator

There is one God and one Mediator who can reconcile God and humanity—the man Christ Jesus. He gave his life to purchase freedom for everyone.

1 TIMOTHY 2:5-6

Micki sank into despair as her marriage unraveled, and in a blur of hopelessness, she took too many antidepressants. She knew she was dying and cried out to Jesus. During her near-death experience, Micki recalls how Jesus advocated for her: "Jesus was standing at the right hand of God, . . . telling God how much I loved him and believed that he died for my sins. God then spoke mentally to me and told me how much he loved me. (Jesus was the mediator between God and me.)"[115]

Jeremy, a lead software engineer, left his body after he had an adverse reaction with alcohol and the medication he was taking. He met Jesus in his NDE and intuitively knew that Jesus was his mediator.

> I was standing in a room with a few people. I will refer to this room as a waiting room but only because I don't have a better explanation for its purpose. It had two opening entranceways to a large courtyard. Everyone knew exactly who I was, and they were definitely waiting for me to arrive. I didn't recognize anyone,

> but I knew they all knew me and loved me. There was one person that was in the room who never said his name, but I knew everything I saw in the building and garden was his.
>
> I am a shy person, so he wanted to show me around, and we went for a walk in the garden section of the courtyard. He introduced me to people in small groups. He knew everyone we met, and they all loved him. I probably was introduced to ten to fifteen people. I remember feeling like I was loved and a sense that everyone longed to meet me.
>
> The whole time, I knew exactly who this man was, and I was so sure of it. He never said who he was; I just knew it. I recognized him as Jesus, not by name but by function. I am terrified of blaspheming, so I hesitate to use this name if there is any evidence that I could be wrong. When I looked at him, I knew he was the mediator to God, [and] the creator, and God. But most of all, I absolutely knew he was the mediator to God in a way that I can't describe. It was just true, and it was so obvious that he was a mediator to God. I don't even know what a mediator to God looks like, but it looks like what I saw.[116]

During Julie's NDE caused by severe bleeding after surgery, she found herself walking and talking with Jesus beside a stream. She recalls:

> There were things that I talked about with Jesus that I did not know or believe at the time. Certain truths that I now know, [like] a person cannot under any circumstances be in the presence of God or anywhere

> near the throne of God without Jesus. It is just not possible. God wants us to be near him and desires it greatly. Jesus is truly the doorway to the throne of God.[117]

. . . .

Jesus is our mediator. A mediator is someone who goes between two parties who are at odds, in order to bring them together, reconciled and united. God acts as his own mediator through Jesus Christ: "For God in all his fullness was pleased to live in Christ, and through him God reconciled everything to himself. He made peace with everything in heaven and on earth by means of Christ's blood on the cross" (Colossians 1:19-20).

As our mediator, Jesus reconciled all that is wrong between us and God and between us and each other, as well as all that is wrong with creation. His role as mediator bridges the divide between how things are and how they should be. We may not feel like we were ever at odds with God, but Scripture tells us otherwise:

> This includes you who . . . were [God's] enemies, separated from him by your evil thoughts and actions. Yet now he has reconciled you to himself through the death of Christ in his physical body. As a result, he has brought you into his own presence, and you are holy and blameless as you stand before him without a single fault.
>
> COLOSSIANS 1:21-22

We have all turned from God in our hearts and minds—by the things we've thought about as well as actions we have committed against his will, for "everyone has sinned; we all fall short of God's glorious standard" (Romans 3:23). Yet through Jesus, God calls all who believe in him "holy and blameless." It's absolutely amazing what Jesus has done for us! If you believe in him, when God looks at you now, he sees you "without a single fault." That's why we can go into God's presence boldly, standing before him with confidence, because we've been reconciled to God by Jesus, our great mediator.

Take some time today to meditate on how Jesus has restored your relationship with God. You are now blameless before God, which means that even in your moments of impatience, jealousy, or anger, you can confidently go to his throne for help. God welcomes you into his presence, so you can boldly come to him for help when you need it most. Through Jesus, your mediator, you are forever reconciled to God and can rest in the promise of his eternal presence.

PRAYER

Holy Father, you say that I'm blameless and without fault because Jesus has reconciled me to you—so you see his payment canceling out all my debts. Thank you that even when I was far from you, you reconciled me as a friend. Thank you that I can boldly come to your throne through Jesus and receive help in my times of need.

38

Righteous Judge

Judge nothing before the appointed time; wait until the Lord comes. He will bring to light what is hidden in darkness and will expose the motives of the heart. At that time each will receive their praise from God.

1 CORINTHIANS 4:5, NIV

While Dean Braxton's body lay dead for an hour and forty-five minutes, Dean was in the presence of God, where he learned many life-altering lessons. Dean was a follower of Christ at the time, and a big lesson he learned was how God wants everyone to be in heaven and is patient for all. He also added that we may be surprised at some of the people we see when we get there.

> People ask me, "Did you think someone in your family would be there that wasn't there?" It wasn't that for me. It was all those I *didn't think* would be there that *were* there! One of them was my Aunt Barbara. You know, I had Aunt Barbara in a whole different place. And there was Aunt Barbara shining—a big smile, and pure joy, and she was in Heaven. I wasn't expecting that. Somewhere in her life she must have made a decision for Jesus. . . . I didn't know when it happened, how it happened, but Jesus did. I came to understand it didn't matter if I knew, it mattered if he knew. . . . We can't judge. I think many of us will find

> many people that we didn't think would make it—make it to Heaven.[118]

Dean goes on to explain his understanding from heaven. God chooses us, and he wants *everyone* to choose him back.

> One of the biggest boxes we have God in is how simple this really is and how difficult we have made it. Jesus has chosen you. He just wants you to choose him. That simple. We put all the other criteria on top of it. He does go after everybody up to their last breath.
>
> What about the person way over here that's never heard of him? I say, "How do you know they haven't ever heard of him?" . . . He's God. I looked into his eyes. I *know* he wants everybody there. It may look different in how he approaches them, but he's going after them.
>
> I don't think there's a person on the planet that does not get that opportunity to make that decision, and it's not a one-time choice. He gives them choice after choice after choice, all the way up to their last breath. I believe God does that for everybody on the planet before they leave the planet.[119]

During her near-death experience due to anaphylactic shock and a five-day coma, critical care nurse Penny Wittbrodt experienced a life review with God. She realized that God alone knows the human heart and each person's backstory, and he alone can righteously judge. As a Christian, she realized she should have listened to people to understand them rather than jump to judgment. Penny recalls what God showed her in her life review:

> Then he shows this negative scene. . . . It was this nurse that I work with, and she was just hard to work with. She wasn't friendly. She was kind of snarky; her patients' call lights would go off forever, . . . so I would end up going in there and getting them off the bed pan or whatever. And I never said anything negative to her, and I always helped her, but I always resented her. . . . And God said, "You're having these thoughts about her," and he shows me her life, and all the things her dad did to her for years—the most horrible molestation and abuse. And I'm like, "Oh my gosh, you know, she's actually killing it in life. She came from this—she never got what she needed in life as far as love and safety and nurturing, and she goes into [nursing] because she wants to give more than she got in a huge way. And you're judging her, and you're thinking negative things about her. You're condemning her in your mind." . . . It occurred to me in that moment, *What if I had taken any of those opportunities to talk to her about her life?* . . . As a Christian, I never even tried to bridge the gap. I was content to just condemn her in my own mind.[120]

....

"God is a righteous judge" (Psalm 7:11, NIV). He alone sees and understands a person's past, their unique influences, choices, intentions, and motivations, as well as their unseen heart and soul. Second Chronicles 16:9 says, "The eyes of the LORD search the whole earth in order to strengthen those whose hearts are fully committed to him." God alone knows every human heart, so he alone can judge rightly. The rest of us are left to judge based only on our limited interactions with a person. We don't know their past, how far they've come, or the heartfelt prayers they've made along the way. That's why Scripture tells us, "Don't make judgments about anyone ahead of time—before the Lord returns. For he will bring our darkest secrets to light and will reveal our private motives. Then God will give to each one whatever praise is due" (1 Corinthians 4:5). God alone knows how to judge rightly, and he will bring justice and reward the unseen motives and deeds done to please him.

As humans, we jump to conclusions about others so quickly. To understand the problem with our relative judgments, it may help to use the analogy of different trees growing over the same amount of time. For instance, we might view someone as godly because of their knowledge and service. This person is comparable to a six-foot-tall tree. Their height is admirable, but we overlook the fact that they started at five feet tall. On the other hand, we might judge someone with seemingly questionable character as "bad" compared to the first person because they have only grown into a one-foot-tall tree. However, God knows that this person started with only six inches of height. So who has really grown the most? Is it the "godly looking" person who has only grown 20 percent, or the spiritually struggling person who has actually doubled in growth over the same time period? God loves and honors *both* for their growth and dedication to becoming more like him, and he alone knows how far each person has come.

The point is that we often judge others based on their outward appearances without knowing what has truly gone on inside their hearts. We can trust that God will take care of their areas of needed growth as he will our own. We can also be confident that if our hearts' desire is to please God, he sees that too and will one day reward it. "There is nothing concealed that will not be disclosed, or hidden that will not be made known" (Matthew 10:26, NIV).

Instead of passing judgment, God wants you to trust his righteous judgment alone. Your role is to partner with God to spur everyone on toward knowing and trusting him more. He is the one who wants all people to be saved and live in his boundless, limitless love.

Today, take some time to reflect on someone you've looked down upon or made judgments about. Ask the Righteous Judge to show you what he sees in that person, and replace your judgmental thoughts with prayers and words of encouragement for them, helping them grow closer to God. Remember, God will cause the growth as they draw nearer to him. And as you focus on growing closer to Jesus yourself, you will naturally become less critical of others and more aware of your own areas of needed growth. *Every* person is in need of being more like Jesus.

PRAYER

Dear God, thank you that you alone judge the human heart. Help me to let go of my judgments of others and instead point others to love and trust you, the one who causes true spiritual growth in us all.

39

Eternal Living Word

The word of God is alive and powerful. It is sharper than the sharpest two-edged sword, cutting between soul and spirit, between joint and marrow. It exposes our innermost thoughts and desires.

HEBREWS 4:12

People who have near-death experiences as followers of Jesus often convey how much Jesus expects us to read, study, and follow his teachings. Randy Kay died after suffering a pulmonary embolism. During Randy's NDE, the Holy Spirit pointed out how knowing God's Word and living it out on earth are directly related to the amount of God's glory people experience in heaven. Randy noticed,

> All people in Heaven walked with a level of radiance about them, but some were brighter than others. The Holy Spirit explained to me that the closer one is to God on earth, the more of God's Glory will shine in and over them. . . . The Holy Spirit directed me to one person who had continuously prayed for people on earth. She had also performed consistent acts of kindness toward others while teaching Bible classes. She gleamed more brightly than those around her. She taught others within a circle, and her command of God's Word and intellectual banter impressed upon

> me that she was a renowned scholar, although the Holy Spirit told me that in the world she had barely graduated from middle school. *She is highly talented and esteemed here because of her faithfulness on earth,* the Holy Spirit whispered.[121]

Dr. Richard Eby was a medical doctor who fell off a two-story balcony, cracked his skull open, and died; yet later he miraculously revived. During his NDE, he asked Jesus some questions, including what kind of life people will live in heaven. Jesus answered him with Scripture and then reminded him of the importance of reading God's Word, saying, "I put it in My book. Didn't you read My book? Everything in it is explanatory of what a child of Mine needs to know." Dr. Eby recalls, "Several times I asked a question and He answered, 'Didn't you read My book?'"[122]

In the conversation Dr. Gary Wood had with Jesus during his NDE from a car crash, Jesus reminded him of the truths of Scripture and how it confounds Jesus when we ignore them:

> Jesus looked right at me with those piercing blue eyes and said, "Don't ever buy the condemnation of the devil that you are unworthy. You are worthy. You have been redeemed by the Blood of the Lamb." He said, "Why do my people not believe in me? Why do my people reject me? Why do they not walk in my commandments?"[123]

....

In Psalm 119:89, the psalmist declares, "Your word, LORD, is eternal; it stands firm in the heavens" (NIV). Peter echoes this truth: "The grass withers and the flower fades. But the word of the Lord remains forever" (1 Peter 1:24-25). All possessions, power, and positions in this world will fade away, but God's Word is eternal; it is inextricably linked to the very person and nature of God. And because of this, his Word is alive and has the power to change the world! God's Word isn't just a philosophy or a set of principles like other religious writings—it has active, *living* power.

"Did you read My book?" is a good question for all of us who claim to follow Jesus. Jesus said, "All who love me will do what I say. My Father will love them, and we will come and make our home with each of them" (John 14:23). Although salvation and relationship with God are not dependent on our deeds, we show our love for God when we follow his commands. It gives him joy when we obey, and it grieves him when we ignore his instruction.

Jesus said, "Man shall not live on bread alone, but on every word that comes from the mouth of God" (Matthew 4:4, NIV). His Word nourishes us, giving us real, proactive energy in life to grow into all he intended for us to be. Jesus prayed for us, "Sanctify them by the truth; your word is truth" (John 17:17, NIV). *Sanctify* means to set apart and purify. God works through his Word to sanctify us—protecting us from the lies of the evil one that constantly try to keep us from experiencing all God wants for us, including the freedom we have in Christ. Jesus said, "If you hold to my teaching, you are really my disciples. Then you will know the truth, and the truth will set you free" (John 8:31-32, NIV).

Jesus is the wisest counselor of all time and the only one who truly knows how life works. When we invest our time in knowing and following his teachings, we will reap rewards in this world and in heaven, because we are investing in something that lasts. There are only three things we can invest in on earth that have eternal value: God, people, and his Word. Regular practices of reading, studying, or meditating on God's Word are very important in deepening our relationship with God. He wants everyone to read his "book"! If you aren't reading his Word regularly, make a commitment to start today, and you will see the difference it makes in your life.

PRAYER

Dear God, thank you for revealing so much of your heart and character through the Bible. Forgive me for not prioritizing your book over so many other books, articles, podcasts, and shows that I go to for wisdom. Today, I want to recommit to knowing you better by reading and doing what you say in your Word.

40

The Way, the Truth, and the Life

Jesus told him, "I am the way, the truth, and the life. No one can come to the Father except through me."

JOHN 14:6

Santosh Acharjee grew up Hindu. In his adult years working as a manufacturing engineer, he didn't think much about faith. After a ruptured pancreas caused his heart to stop, the doctor put him in a medically induced coma, where he remained on machines for three days and nights. Santosh clinically died, and when he came back, he was never the same again.

> I always thought that once you die, your life is finished. That's it. But when I died, I discovered your life isn't over, there's another life after that. . . . I saw a bright Light coming toward me. . . . I knew that this Light has superior authority—I had to obey that Light; no one had to tell me, I just knew. When the Light came near me, I could then see my body on the hospital bed. The Light engulfed me with his radiance, and all that I could see was the Divine Light. He was taking me some place, but I immediately fell in love with the Divine Light. I knew the Light's purpose was not to harm me but [to] protect me. . . . I was

> following the Light and when he stopped, he stopped like the sun over this beautiful compound. I'm trying to figure out, what is this place?
>
> I looked to the center of this platform [I was on], and I saw that there were three steps, each seven feet high, like an altar, and on the top was a huge throne. And on this throne, it looked like somebody was sitting there. When I looked, I saw the Lord Almighty. I didn't know who He was except that He was God. I didn't have to ask or find out; I knew this was Lord of everything, Lord of all. I looked at this face only once, but I could not look a second time because shame and guilt overcame me. I had committed so many sins, and when I looked at Him, every sin I had ever committed was flashed before my eyes. I could not look at His face, and kept repeating, "Lord, please forgive me. Lord, please forgive me. I committed so many wrongdoings in my life; please forgive me." . . .
>
> Then the Lord spoke to me, in a deep authoritative voice, yet it had so much love and compassion. . . . He said, "I'm sending you back to the earth."[124]

The Lord sent Santosh back. The doctors were all amazed at how Santosh miraculously recovered from multiple terminal complications. But Santosh's life had been upended. He sought God from that point forward, asking God to show him the Truth and the Way. And just as God promises to be found by those who seek him, Santosh came to faith in Jesus two years later. Santosh shares, "I realized that [He] was none other than Jesus Christ [whom] I met in Heaven. Jesus is the one we can meet in the human form of God. And I realized God *is* love—that's what I experienced, and it's what I read in the Bible."[125]

Dr. Rajiv Parti was a chief anesthesiologist who thought NDEs were psychosis, until he had one. Afterward, he sought to know the identity of the God of Light he encountered. He had a vision of his friend with this God of Light the very night his friend died.

> I felt the presence of the Being of Light, the same Being I had encountered during my NDE. This time, however, a Being emerged from the Light, a tall man with a pale-brown complexion and a beard, wearing a majestic white gown. Most memorable were his deep blue eyes. He was radiating unconditional love. "Who are you?" I asked the Being. "I am Jesus, your savior," he responded.[126]

....

Scripture teaches that every person in the world will meet God when they leave this earth (see Revelation 1:7), and this does mean *all* people—regardless of their faith background or current beliefs. And initially, in God's presence, every person will feel his essence and his love because God *is* love—he can't *not* love. Yet those who return still have the opportunity to make a choice to seek God and find out who he is.

God promises that "you will find him if you seek him with all your heart and with all your soul" (Deuteronomy 4:29, NIV). But he gives you free will to choose to love him and follow him, or to go your own way. As John 14:6 says, Jesus is "the way, the truth, and the life," and through Jesus, all people have the opportunity to be reconciled to God. As Santosh realized, Jesus is the unseen God revealed in human form. He is the way to God because he paid the price for all our sins to be forgiven, so that every willing heart can be restored to right relationship with God.

Jesus is the source of true transformation and hope for all people, and he promises to give you an abundant life as you learn from him, walking in his grace, mercy, and love. There is no greater truth to live by and no higher life to seek than the Way of Jesus. Today, meditate on Jesus as *your* way, *your* truth, and *your* life. Take some time to focus on allowing him to have his will and ways in you more and more every day, and watch how this brings fresh joy and abundance to your life.

PRAYER

Dear Jesus, you are the Way and the Truth that leads to the Life of purpose and love you created me to live. There is no other God but you. Help me to live out your will and ways as I stay true to you, for nothing else satisfies my deepest longings.

41

Jesus, Our Salvation

"Joseph, son of David," the angel said, "do not be afraid to take Mary as your wife. . . . She will have a son, and you are to name him Jesus, for he will save his people from their sins."

MATTHEW 1:20-21

Dean Braxton had been pronounced dead for an hour and forty-five minutes, yet miraculously revived. During his near-death experience, Dean was filled with gratitude as he found himself in the presence of Jesus, feeling the fullness of his salvation in a very tangible way.

> I found myself leaving my body and going toward this Light that was ahead of me. . . . I knew that was where Jesus and the Father were, and when I came in, I realized everything was right. There was nothing wrong. . . . The thing I love to say is, "I fit." "I fit here."
>
> When I first came in, there was a forest right before me. Not only did I feel like everything was right and there was nothing wrong, I felt so welcomed, and so accepted by everything. The whole atmosphere accepted me. Every creation there accepted me. I can't even describe the feeling—it was *past* peace.
>
> I wanted to be where Jesus is and I knew he was through this forest; I just knew it. . . . The trees

> opened up and as I was going through the forest, I could hear everything saying, "He's going to see the King." The flowers, the grass, even the clouds and atmosphere were saying it.
>
> And as I came out, there was Jesus, and before him was this great congregation. . . . He was facing this crowd, like in a meadow is the closest I can describe it. I remember he was to the left of me, and I went over where he was, and I went down on my hands and knees, . . . and I said these words, "You did this for me?" And the next thing was, "Thank you, thank you, thank you."
>
> What was going through my thoughts and my heart at that time was, *The only reason I was there was because of what he had done.* My good works didn't get me in and my bad works didn't keep me out. . . . It was what *he* had done.[127]

In his NDE after his twin-engine plane crashed, Captain Dale Black found himself guided through the holy city, up toward the light in the city center to the throne of God. There he experienced how his salvation granted him authority to be in this wonderful place:

> I had been ushered closer and closer toward the light. . . . Then there was a stairway that was near a glass sea, which did look like a sea, . . . that went up, and a large angel with the most power (if we could say that) moved just to the side. Just behind this angel was another individual, and all I saw were the eyes. And the eyes were just looking at me, . . . and the eyes were penetrating, to say the least. But I looked into the eyes

> of the warmest, kindest, most wonderful [person]—I knew this was the Son of God. I knew this was my Savior! And all of a sudden, my knees buckled, my legs lost their strength, and I just went down. I couldn't stand. I was not worthy to stand in his presence. . . . I was somehow granted this authority [and] had this supernatural gift that I was worthy. Somebody had done something for me.[128]

....

The angel Gabriel instructed Jesus' father, Joseph, before Jesus' birth: "You are to name him Jesus, for he will save his people" (Matthew 1:21). *Yeshua*, the Hebrew name for Jesus, is derived from two Hebrew words: *Ya*, short for Yahweh, and *yasha*, which means "to deliver," "to save." So the name Jesus, *Yeshua*, literally means, "Yahweh saves" or "Yahweh is salvation." It's fascinating to realize that throughout the Old Testament, long before Jesus was born, when David or the prophets proclaimed, "The Lord is my salvation," they were unknowingly proclaiming, in a sense, the name of Jesus, *Ya-shua*, "Yahweh is salvation."

God foretold that his salvation through Jesus would come to provide forgiveness of sins and so much more. "But even greater is God's wonderful grace and his gift of righteousness, for all who receive it will live in triumph over sin and death through this one man, Jesus Christ" (Romans 5:17). For believers, salvation includes forgiveness and the restoration of things as they were meant to be—the inheritance of our lives restored—where we are made worthy by God to belong and feel accepted, loved, and in harmony with all of creation.

Today, take time to meditate on the fullness of this gift of salvation. God has saved you and forgiven you. He heals your wounds, loves you unconditionally, and restores all that you've lost. As you imagine the fullness of your salvation, think about the name that made it possible—the name above all names—the name *Jesus*. Our good deeds cannot earn our salvation, and our mistakes cannot negate God's greatest gift. Let this motivate you to worship and follow Jesus in full obedience, for he is our salvation!

PRAYER

Jesus, you are Yeshua, and your name is above all names. You alone are my salvation, and I thank you for all you have done for me. Continue to restore my life to all you intend it to be, as I live out the fullness of my salvation in you.

42

Extravagant Goodness

"Good Teacher, what must I do to inherit eternal life?"
"Why do you call me good?" Jesus asked. "Only God is truly good."
MARK 10:17-18

While living a life of partying in college, Cedric Pisegna was not what he would have called "good." Yet during his near-death experience, he encountered the goodness of God, which ultimately led him to turn his life completely around and become a Passionist priest. He also found resolve to our toughest questions about a good God:

> Like everyone else, I question, "How can a good God allow all of this to occur? Why doesn't God step in and stop this?" . . . When I stood in God's presence, all of my questioning melted away! As I reflect on this now, I am shocked by this truth, but it is real. The only way to put it is, "I knew even as I was known!" All of the tragedies, sufferings and unanswered questions melt away in the presence of our glorious God.[129]
>
> As my journey unfolded, I realized he is my good Shepherd, [due to] the fact that he would put his arm around a twenty-year-old's shoulder who had had an abortion, and he would treat me like an intimate

> friend. He's a friend of the outcast, the marginalized, the poor. It was Jesus—because of *his* passion—that I was summoned to the Throne of God.[130] . . . God's care and affection for me were not conditioned on my goodness; rather, there was such powerful, pulsating goodness radiating from God that it was overwhelming.[131]

When commercial airline pilot Jim Woodford died of an accidental opioid overdose, he cried out to God and found himself walking in the outskirts of heaven. Jim learned a valuable lesson from his guardian angel, Skysong, about the goodness of God and how God sees our world. Jim was struck by how we, as image-bearers of God, can reflect God's goodness on earth.

> I asked the angel, "Skysong, I just don't understand. I wake up in the morning and I turn on the news, and it doesn't matter what network, I see the chaos of the night before."
>
> I asked Skysong, "Why doesn't God give up on us? What does he possibly see in us?"
>
> He looked down at me with those beautiful violet eyes and said, "James, do you not know, that what God sees in you and mankind is himself? He will *never* give up on you."
>
> And then he did the most amazing thing. He said, "With all your technology, you have the ability to instantaneously send or receive messages anywhere in the world, yet your news programs never mention the billions of acts of kindness that occur every day that we see and celebrate in Heaven. No one will send a news crew to your home because you shoveled the walk of

> your neighbor, or you helped an elderly person get their groceries, or you volunteered at a food kitchen. They do not report that."
>
> He said, "What I want you to keep in mind, James, is to never lose heart. Because if you take all the goodness that happens at every moment of every hour of every day on earth—this is the goodness that happens every second on earth (he made a huge globe with his arms and wings) and this is the evil (he made a tiny point with his fingers)."
>
> We have to remember kindness is inherent in most of us. It's *God's* kindness. And it's our duty—our gift back to God.[132]

....

God is good. In fact, he *defines* what goodness is, which is why Jesus said, "No one is good except God alone" (Mark 10:18, ESV). God acts for the good of all people at all times, and even those who oppose him are recipients of his goodness. Because God is the essence of what "good" is and does, all our acts of "doing good" merely reflect God's image in us.

So, what is God's goodness like? Micah the prophet declares, "The LORD has told you what is good: . . . to do what is right, to love mercy, and to walk humbly with your God" (Micah 6:8). God loves righteousness, mercy, and humility—these reflect his goodness. Jesus describes God's extravagant goodness when he tells us how we can be like our heavenly Father: "Do good to those who hate you. Bless those who curse you. Pray for those who hurt you" (Luke 6:27-28). God sets this example through Jesus, and when we are good to those who don't deserve it, we reflect his image on earth. Jesus promises that when you show his goodness to others, "then your reward from heaven will be very great, and you will truly be acting as children of the Most High" (Luke 6:35).

Take some time today to be mindful of how you can show God's extravagant goodness to others. Include both the small, seemingly insignificant acts of kindness that only heaven notices, and the unconventional ways of blessing those who may seem undeserving of your kindness. As you share God's heart of grace and mercy, you will find that his goodness will expand even more in you. Imagine the smile on Jesus' face as all of heaven celebrates your displays of God's goodness to the world!

PRAYER

Dear God, you alone are good. Show me how to radiate your goodness and love to the world through purposeful acts of kindness toward all people. Help me pray for those against me, bless those who curse me, and do good to everyone, whether I think they deserve it or not. I want the world to experience your extravagant goodness and love through me.

43

The Powerful Word

In the beginning the Word already existed. The Word was with God, and the Word was God. He existed in the beginning with God. God created everything through him, and nothing was created except through him. The Word gave life to everything that was created, and his life brought light to everyone.

JOHN 1:1-4

While Randy Kay was without a pulse for thirty minutes, Jesus took him before the throne of God the Father, where he learned about the power and authority of God's Word.

> I could not see the outline of the Father's face because of the brilliance of the light upon him. . . . "You see the Father," said the Holy Spirit. . . . "His is the Word, beloved, and before Jesus walked the earth, the three of Us abided as the Word. . . . And the Word spoke life, and the Word spoke truth, and the Word spoke the way, and the order of these things was established first on earth. . . ." Although these words may sound confusing to those in the flesh, they made perfect sense to me in Heaven as I recalled the words in the Book of Life as first recorded by John: "The Word became flesh and made his dwelling among us. We have seen his glory, the glory of the one and only Son, who came from the Father, full of grace and truth" (John 1:14, NIV).[133]

The Word of God powerfully created all that exists, including humans who were created in God's image. That's why our words also have incredible power—power to give life or destroy it. As Kevin Zadai went under anesthesia during dental surgery, something went terribly wrong. Next thing he knew, Kevin was watching the surgery from above as Jesus taught him about the power of his words and the words that had shaped him throughout his life. Jesus told him, "Your words are very, very powerful."[134] Kevin goes on to say,

> [Jesus] said, "Kevin, in Matthew 12:36, I said that you will be held accountable for every idle word that comes out of your mouth." He said, "You know I meant that." And he started to speak to me about how I had been very careless about my words. . . . Jesus said, "You're supposed to be speaking where you're going." And it was very uncomfortable at first because he said that I wasn't being careful with my words. . . . [But] he cared about me, and he showed me how my life up to that point had been going in a zigzag. . . .
>
> Then he said, "When you [were] born again, Kevin, the Spirit of God inside of you made you new. You're a brand-new creature now. Now that your spirit is new, you have to speak from your spirit. . . . Kevin, when you pray in the Spirit, when you speak the right words, the demons have to listen to you." . . . And I realized, *Oh my gosh, this is what's been going wrong in my life. I haven't been speaking the right things.*[135]

....

The apostle John tells us that Jesus is the Word of God (see John 1:1). The Greek term translated "word" here is *logos*, a term that often carries the meaning of "speech" (the spoken word). John explains that this Word, Jesus, existed with God in the beginning and was the creative spoken force of God who brought everything to life.

As beings created in God's image, the words we speak also hold incredible creative power and can shape our reality too. We should be very careful of the words we say and choose them wisely. Proverbs 18:21 warns us that "the tongue can bring death or life," so our words can be used for building people up or tearing them down. Life-giving words are aligned with God's heart; careless and demeaning words are against it. One day we will stand accountable for every word spoken, as well as their ripple effects, good or bad.

In our humanity, we tend to amplify our negative thoughts about others and situations, often criticizing instead of encouraging people, even those we love the most. However, our speech should strive to reflect the fruit of the Spirit: "love, joy, peace, patience, kindness, goodness, faithfulness, gentleness, and self-control" (Galatians 5:22-23). When we do this, our words reflect the heart of God, creating a ripple effect of powerful, positive impact in the world. When we don't align our words with God's heart, the ripple effect is just as strong and will negatively affect the world in destructive ways in the process.

Today, purposefully use your words to bless and encourage those around you, especially people you tend to criticize or find fault with—including yourself. Ask God to reveal positive and uplifting words that you can speak over people, and feel the life-giving power it brings when you say them. Remember,

God sees potential and purpose in each person, so take seriously the power he has given you to build up and bless through your words. Choose now to speak life into every situation, and you will experience the joy of the Word working in you and through you to make a positive impact in the world.

PRAYER

God, you are the powerful, living Word. Thank you for speaking life over me and blessing me forward. Help me to choose my words wisely and commit to encouraging and building people up, creating a positive life-giving force for good in my relationships.

44

Triune God

Hear, O Israel: The LORD our God, the LORD is one.

DEUTERONOMY 6:4, NIV

Although the term *Trinity* is not explicitly mentioned in the Bible, the revelation of God's triune nature is clear. And people who have had near-death experiences can help us better imagine this mystery that goes beyond our finite understanding. Dean Braxton, who was clinically dead for an hour and forty-five minutes, recalls,

> When I first came upon Jesus, I knew all of a sudden that the Holy Spirit, Jesus, and the Father are one. It was just an inward knowing that I was not speaking to one, but all three at the same time. And most of the speaking was not verbal, but thought-to-thought, and as I was speaking in my head, I was aware of each distinct person there hearing, but they were one. Not like we would think of one; I knew the fullness of Jesus was in the Father, and the fullness of the Holy Spirit was in Jesus—I could not separate them there. I have to separate them now, so it sounds like I was just talking to Jesus, but I knew I was talking to Father

> and Holy Spirit. I did experience Jesus, the glorified man, and then the Father on his throne, but I realized there is a box we've built around it, that the actual experience transcends our words. God the Father is, as the Bible says, a Spirit. He is pure Spirit. He is pure love, and he is pure life, and he is pure light! . . . All I can say is there is no end to God the Father. He is bright like Jesus with many colors coming off of him. Jesus and the Father God light up everything.[136]
>
> People say the "Trinity" is Father, Son, Holy Spirit. No one thinks that way there. They're just one. Even trying to answer this question for you, I'm trying to put something in earthly terms, but in Heaven, the question doesn't exist.[137]

As Randy Kay's body lay without heartbeat for thirty minutes, Randy experienced a different relational aspect of the Father, Son, and Spirit in heaven:

> Initially I thought [Jesus] was speaking to me both without words and speaking to me audibly. And because Jesus and the Holy Spirit were One, I came to realize, . . . he was speaking to me both ways, audibly and without words, but the times I heard him without words, in understanding, that was the Holy Spirit. I realized at the time that Jesus was my friend, my companion, but my most intimate relationship was through the Holy Spirit. . . . So Jesus, during the course of our walk, said, "I am going to take you to the Throne Room." . . . I realized there was an intensity in where he was taking me. . . . I was being brought to the Father. And the kinship I felt with Jesus, and the intimacy I

> felt with the Holy Spirit, now was being taken to a new place in this sympatico relationship that they had, both separate and together. . . . Jesus pointed to the Throne. And it wasn't like a chair; that's not what it was like. This was a place . . . where this figure appeared. He was gargantuan in size, . . . a building-size figure. And his appearance was very different in that I could not see his face. . . . Jesus was standing by me, and he was with the Father at the same time. . . . It made perfect sense to me [in Heaven]. . . . The Father—I perceived him as the Creator. Jesus was my friend, my companion. . . . The Holy Spirit was my comforter; he was the one always with me.[138]

. . . .

The concept of God's triune nature may seem paradoxical to us, especially while we are confined to a three-dimensional world. However, seeking to understand and appreciate it can lead to a deeper connection with God.

God the *Father* reminds us that he is all-powerful and the ultimate authority to lead and guide us. He is the creator of all things, so he can accomplish all things. His love for you is perfect, protective, and entirely unique, like a parent's love for their child. There's nothing he wouldn't do for you, and there's nothing he can't do.

Jesus, the *Son*, revealed God in human form, and shows us that our almighty, infinite, eternal Father understands us completely. God united with his beloved creation through his Son, Jesus. This is an astounding thought—God intimately joined himself to humanity forever! Jesus experienced humanity, from infancy into adulthood, going through all the challenges we face here on earth. Jesus still has the scars on his resurrected body, reminding us that God intimately understands all we've been through, because he felt the weight of all our hurt, pain, sin, and shame on himself when he died on the cross. He loves each one of us unconditionally in a deeply personal way.

The *Holy Spirit* is a powerful reminder that God's presence is always with us, comforting us and producing spiritual fruit, as we listen and respond to his voice speaking to our thoughts. God the Father and Jesus are living inside us by the Holy Spirit, as Jesus explained in John 14:16-17, 20: "I will ask the Father, and he will give you another Advocate, who will never leave you. He is the Holy Spirit. . . . [And] you will know that I am in my Father, and you are in me, and I am in you." The Holy Spirit is our intimate companion and the source of God's peace in our lives, praying for us, guiding us, comforting us, and filling us with God's presence.

Today, try to expand your imagination and include the complete essence of the triune God in your relationship with him. Whether you need guidance from the Father, love from the Son, or comfort from the Spirit, focus on the different persons of God according to your needs, while acknowledging the mystery that God is one. This moment, embrace the depth and breadth of God's limitless, boundless love reflected in his triune nature.

PRAYER

Dear God, thank you for your triune essence that meets all my needs. God the Father, I'm so grateful that I'm in your protective hands. I trust you. Thank you, Jesus, for showing me the Truth and the Way. I want to follow you. And thank you, Holy Spirit, for your presence in my life—I want to listen to your voice and grow spiritual fruit to bless those around me.

45

God Enjoys Us

You make known to me the path of life;
you will fill me with joy in your presence,
with eternal pleasures at your right hand.

PSALM 16:11, NIV

Heidi Barr was an adventurous teenager who loved racing down the mountains bareback on her horse. The day her horse fell on her and crushed her, Jesus took her on the ride of her life during her near-death experience. She later reflected how Jesus knew precisely what would thrill her sixteen-year-old heart.

> Jesus took my hand, and like Superman and Lois Lane, off we flew. He and I left the scene of my death. It wasn't quite flying, although I did stretch out my left arm like a bird's wing. What we did together was surf. Jesus took me surfing, body surfing, on a wave of light. It was the most fun experience in the history of the world! I looked down, and I could see a wave of light rolling beneath our bare feet, pushing us forward, faster and faster. The light was made of all colors. I laughed as I felt it tickling the bottoms of my feet. . . . As I stretched out my arm, I could feel the light flow through my fingers like water. This was great. Jesus was great. He and I were laughing out loud as we surfed. His smile was so wide and there

> was such a mischievous sparkle in his eyes. His sense of fun was contagious! He loved having the ability to gift this experience to me, to share this experience with me. I was awed by his power and his laughter and his joy as we journeyed together.[139]

It may be hard to imagine God enjoying us, yet multiple people with NDEs confirm it is true. At age fourteen, Sarah was in a severe car accident that caused her NDE. Just like Heidi, she had a similar thrilling encounter with Jesus as they were coming back to earth from heaven (which she calls "HOME"):

> Jesus and I left all the people. . . . We left Home behind and set off back to earth. I remember it was so fast and yet I knew we traveled a great distance. . . . I looked at the water of Earth and wanted to see the water. Then WHOOSH, just like that, we were flying so fast, it was awesome. I was smiling like I have never before. Like a roller-coaster ride, but a million times better. There was no fear of heights or falling. It was a ride I will never forget. . . . I skimmed across the top of the water and laughed as we flew away back to the hospital. I took one last look around before going back in this body.[140]

A while ago, a medical doctor and his wife came up after our church service one Sunday, introduced themselves, and explained what brought them to our church and to faith in Jesus. Their four-year-old son had come close to death several times in the hospital due to medical issues. They had both been agnostic and never talked about God or Jesus with their son. They shared that one night their son began saying, "I want to go run and play with Jesus in the field again." They were confused by this, but after multiple nights of their son wishing to play with Jesus, they finally asked him, "When did you run and play with Jesus?" The little boy said, "When he came and got me from the hospital."

....

Many people do not realize that God is the most joyful being imaginable. Not only is God the source of all joy, but God takes pleasure in fun, and he even delights in us. God created us in his image—with the ability to enjoy life, experience pleasure, and utilize our creative gifts to invent endless games, sports, and thrilling adventures! Since God is responsible for all our delight and enjoyment, why would we think he is any less capable of enjoying us enjoying all his good gifts?

We love giving gifts to our children and then experiencing their enjoyment with them, playing and delighting in their fun and laughter. Of course, God would never be less of a wonderful parent to his children than we are to ours! In fact, God commanded the people of Israel to celebrate with joy in his presence at the annual Festival of Shelters: "Celebrate with joy before the LORD your God for seven days" (Leviticus 23:40).

Do you imagine God brimming with joy and laughter, as someone who finds pleasure and delight alongside his children? Try to imagine God delighting in you today as you enjoy life with him, and thank him throughout your day for everything that makes your heart smile. Acknowledge that he is your ultimate source of true joy and lasting happiness, now and forever. As you invite him into your fun and delight, picture him beaming as he enjoys you enjoying him!

PRAYER

Dear God, thank you that you delight in me as your child! I want to invite you into my moments of joy and fun so that we can experience them together. I know that you are the giver and source of all genuine joy and happiness, and I praise you! I'm so grateful that my joy brings joy to your heart.

46

The Narrow Gate

Yes, I am the gate. Those who come in through me will be saved.
They will come and go freely and will find good pastures.
The thief's purpose is to steal and kill and destroy.
My purpose is to give them a rich and satisfying life.

JOHN 10:9-10

It is fascinating that many people who have near-death experiences receive parables from God during their heavenly encounters. As a Hindu, Santosh Acharjee thought that when he died, he would come back as another living thing. To his surprise, when his pancreas ruptured and his heart stopped, that did not happen. Instead, a loving Divine Light appeared and took him to a place overlooking the splendor of the Kingdom of Heaven. He saw twelve gates into this spectacular city that he longed to enter, but the gates appeared closed to him. He was afraid until the Lord spoke to him.

> Then the Lord spoke to me in a deep authoritative voice, yet it had so much love and compassion. . . . He said, "I'm sending you back to the earth, but when I send you back, I want you to love your family and love your children." I was afraid, and I was thinking of the worst, but when He spoke, I could hear the tenderness, the mercy, and [the] compassion in His voice.

> When I was looking at his feet, on his left side [my right] I saw that there was a very narrow door, like a narrow gate, and that was the only gate open to me—that narrow gate. All others were closed, but this narrow door was open, and through it I could see [into] the Kingdom of Heaven.[141]
>
> Hearing the loving and caring voice of the Lord, I gathered a little more courage, and I asked, "Lord! I'm not worthy of standing before You. I'm a sinner! I've sinned, Lord! How can I be sure that I can enter through this narrow door next time?"[142] . . .
>
> The Lord said, "Do not be afraid. I will be with you, and I will guide you." By then, I noticed that I was not feeling afraid of God anymore. To me, He was very kind, loving, and like a true friend with genuine concern for each and every one of us.[143]

When Santosh returned to earth, he sought this God of love and mercy, praying daily to know who this God was and how to enter the narrow gate. Two years later, his daughter was invited to sing in a church (she was a choral major in college). When Santosh entered the church to hear his daughter, he felt the same loving presence of the Almighty he had encountered in heaven. The message that day was based on Matthew 7:13: "You can enter God's Kingdom only through the narrow gate," and John 10:9, where Jesus declares, "I am the gate. Those who come in through me will be saved." Santosh knew this message was for him. He went home and began reading the Bible and said, "All I experienced was in this book." He became a follower of Jesus, the one who *is* the gate through which we enter the Kingdom of Heaven.[144]

....

Jesus called himself the Gate. During his earthly ministry, Jesus loved teaching in parables. He would often use metaphors or analogies when teaching about God's Kingdom, but many people didn't like his parabolic ways of communicating. However, he was testing their hearts for a reason. God often tests us to see if we will really seek him and put thought and effort into understanding his wisdom and ways. God gave Santosh a parable-like vision of a narrow gate leading into the Kingdom of Heaven. When Santosh did sincerely seek God's guidance, he was led to the truth. "'You will seek me and find me when you seek me with all your heart. . . .' declares the Lord" (Jeremiah 29:13-14, NIV).

It is so easy for us to get frustrated with God when he doesn't just tell us the answer or give us a script to follow. It's important to remember that the Lord is a parable-telling God. He wants to see if we will seek to understand and follow him in the narrow way. In John 10:7, Jesus said, "I am the gate for the sheep." He is the provision through which we find forgiveness of sins to enter a relationship with God, but he is also the gate through which we find "good pastures" and "a rich and satisfying life" (John 10:9-10).

Do you patiently and diligently seek God's wisdom, trusting he will lead you into a rich and satisfying life, or do you find yourself quickly detouring to other pastures in search of the "good life?" Do you follow the crowd when they tell you they have the way to true life and happiness, doing what feels good in the moment? These options may look alluring and exciting, yet as Jesus indicated, the broad path ends up stealing, killing, and destroying the life we really want.

Jesus is the gate that leads to life. His ways might seem narrow and restrictive at first, but they lead to open pastures of spiritual abundance on the other side. Be assured that God is so compassionate and merciful that even when we detour from his will out of impatience, as soon as we turn back to him, he opens the gate to lead us into better pastures. Take a moment today to talk to God about the areas in your life where you've detoured away from the good he desires for you. He is there right now to listen and guide you as you seek his wisdom. Through Jesus, the gate to good pastures is always before you.

PRAYER

Lord, you are the gate to life. Forgive me when I get impatient and turn from you when I don't understand your ways immediately or when things get confusing. I want to seek you and your wisdom with all my heart. Give me strength to go through your gate that leads to abundant life.

47

Our True Home

Lord, through all the generations you have been our home!

PSALM 90:1

Many who have had near-death experiences have discovered that God in heaven is our true home. They have seen how families can finally be restored and reunited as the family of God. After dying from pneumonia in the 1890s, Rebecca Springer remembers Frank, her deceased brother-in-law, showing her a gorgeous house in heaven crafted and decorated just for her tastes. Then another joyful surprise awaited her inside.

> Advancing up the long room to meet me, I saw my dear father and mother, and with them my youngest sister. With a cry of joy, I flew into my father's outstretched arms, and heard, with a thrill of joy, his dear, familiar "My precious little daughter!"
>
> "At last! At last!" I cried, clinging to him. "At last I have you again!"
>
> "At last!" he echoed, with a deep-drawn breath of joy. Then he resigned me to my dear mother, and we were soon clasped in each other's embrace. . . . Oh, what an hour was that! I did not dream that even heaven could hold such joy.[145]

When doctors could not revive Dean Braxton's body from organ failure, Dean found himself fully alive in heaven, meeting generations of ancestors. He saw clearly how God loves the earthly family he chose for him, and he realized all our family issues resolve when we are home in heaven:

> About fifteen to twenty feet away, I noticed all these beings, people, . . . my family. My grandmother Mary was standing out front, and behind her were other family members, and behind them was generation after generation after generation. It went back so far. I thought to myself later on: *Family is important to God.*
>
> People ask me what they looked like. They were shining, had a big smile and pure joy. The reason they were shining is because Jesus was shining out of them. The reason they were smiling is there were no worries. You know you're in Heaven when the whole family is smiling![146]

Karina Martinez felt unworthy to enter heaven the day her pacemaker failed. Jesus told her she *was* worthy (she had just prayed to him for forgiveness, by which *he* makes us worthy). She was still unsure if she was welcome, so she asked Jesus if he would show her some family members to reassure her. He said, "Look!"

> I saw my Max, my beautiful dog Max, that I had lost the day before getting my pacemaker. And I saw my other dog, Tasha, who had died. And I opened my eyes fully and was so full of joy, I just went right in. I was so happy. I ran after my dog, and then I started just flying. When I was there, I was flying, flying, and

> flying. And I saw this tree, this beautiful, beautiful tree with purple flowers, with this radiant white light going through the roots. It was by a river. I flew above this beautiful garden, and I could see golden streets, but light coming out of them, so they looked like shiny glass almost. And there was a city with structures—gorgeous. I was home. I knew this was my true home, and it filled my heart with joy.[147]

....

Home is where we belong! In heaven, we will feel fully known, accepted, celebrated, and loved, just for who we are. Here on earth, we only get tastes of what it feels like to be fully at home. Home is a place of safety, caring, connection, and joy with the ones who have been with us through life. Unfortunately, some people may grow up without ever feeling any sense of home. Others may have wonderful childhoods but soon discover that this feeling of "home" gets attacked and destroyed in this world.

In God's house, we are truly home because God *is* our true home. And in heaven, God's love, joy, and acceptance will permeate our very beings, shining out of all of us with the love and light of God. That's why the Bible assures us that we will share in God's glory (see Colossians 3:4). And in the light of God's glory in heaven, all families will find healing and all divisions or estrangements will be reconciled.

Scripture tells us we are all in God's family as believers, even now:

> All of us can come to the Father through the same Holy Spirit because of what Christ has done for us. . . . You are members of God's family. . . . And the

cornerstone is Christ Jesus himself. We are carefully joined together in him.

EPHESIANS 2:18-21

Today, take a moment to reflect on what it means to be part of God's family, a family where you always belong. Ask God how you can love others this way even now, helping them feel accepted and secure in belonging, just like in heaven—where everyone will say, "I'm finally home!"

PRAYER

Father in heaven, how grateful I am that you call me your child. Thank you that in heaven I am loved and accepted in your family forever. I pray that all of my family will know you as Father too. Help me extend your love, acceptance, and sense of belonging to everyone in my path until we are all home with you.

48

Tenderhearted Mercy

The Lord is full of tenderness and mercy.

JAMES 5:11

Jim Woodford was a wealthy commercial airline pilot who never prayed a day in his life. But as he was dying of an accidental opioid overdose, he cried out to God for forgiveness. Not only did he discover a mercy he did not deserve, but he also met a God whose tenderhearted kindness extends to all who will receive it.

Jim remembers his guardian angel guiding him through heaven's magnificent beauty, when the angel said, "James, touch my robe."

> I did, and instantly we were in the sky. . . . I was looking down on this golden city, and instantaneously I knew I was looking down on God's celestial home. I was able to see these magnificent buildings; the Halls of Knowledge, the Halls of Learning, the Halls of Music . . . they were hewn from blocks of light, not stone. So they had a warmth that radiated from them. . . .
>
> But there was this one building that had the most beautiful aura about it. And there was a huge green space around it. And I said, "What is this building?"

and the Guardian said, "James, that is the nursery." And I said "Nursery? A nursery in Heaven?' and he looked at me and smiled, and said, "Yes, James. That is the nursery. This is where the souls of aborted children, or children that have died in their innocence from disease or sickness [or] during childbirth are cared for. And God so loves their light, and we gather it [their light] back, and they're raised in the nursery. They're not growing a mortal body, and they grow three times as fast as they did on earth. Many of them stay on and help in the nursery or join their families that have gone before them into Heaven or wait for their moms to come."

And you know, of all the things I talk about—I've had so many women come up to me in tears, saying that "forty years ago I had an abortion . . . I've regretted it all my life . . . now I know my child waits for me." And they do. I mean we serve the most merciful of Supreme Beings we could ever hope to have. And he sees the hurt in the soul and what that lady carried in her heart all these years, yearning for her children. It speaks to the mercy of God; the love of God.[148]

As Randy Kay walked with Jesus through the dazzling landscape of heaven after he died, Jesus had something similar to show him.

Jesus motioned to my right. Flowing down from a mountain was a waterfall that appeared to be made of white linens that rippled like waters, with the sound of hundreds of flapping flags that evoked the intoxicating aroma of a newborn. The flowing ripples met the base

> of the ground and appeared as satiny white waves. . . . Atop these waves frolicked thousands of children and newborns, along with completely white angels whose gowns seemed to flow with the linens. Shouts of joy ushered from the mouths of the children and newborns. Giggles abounded from this place, as the angels bounced with the children the way an inflatable bounce house magnifies joy at a child's birthday party. . . .
>
> "You see those who died as young children, and the unborn of the world," Jesus said.
>
> His words struck me with the gravity of what brought these children to Heaven, especially knowing that many appeared before me who had been aborted in the world. But even that awareness did not sadden me, because God had redeemed their childhood in Heaven, restoring the absolute fun and feelings of blissful abandonment they had lost on earth. Even now, I tell mothers who aborted their babies and who felt guilty afterward that God restores their baby's joy in Heaven.[149]

. . . .

God's immense, tenderhearted mercy toward all who turn to him for forgiveness will always be within reach, no matter what the circumstance. King David committed adultery, then tried to cover it up by having Bathsheba's husband killed in battle. In Psalm 51, David cried out, "Have mercy on me, O God, because of your unfailing love. Because of your great compassion, blot out the stain of my sins. Wash me clean from my guilt. Purify me from my sin" (verses 1-2). David's sin was great, yet God's mercy was greater. And despite what David did, God forgave him and later called David "a man after my own heart"

(Acts 13:22) because he humbled himself, confessed his wrongs, and turned back to follow God. Though our sins still can have serious consequences in this life, as David also experienced, God's mercy makes a path forward.

Because of God's great mercy and his tender heart toward all his children, God is always working to restore what our broken, evil world tries to destroy. As we turn toward him and allow ourselves to be embraced by his compassion and unconditional love for us, God returns joy and innocence to all his children, including you—no matter what you've done. As you lean on God's vast tenderhearted mercy toward you, you'll feel restoration and wholeness begin to grow in your heart.

Maybe you've lost a child to miscarriage, a tragedy, or abortion, and you've suffered greatly. God has tenderhearted mercy and love for your child *and* for you—you are also his child. Imagine God restoring joy to your child in heaven right now, with assurance that one day you will reunite with your child again. In gratitude, praise God for his loving-kindness, forgiveness, and the restoration of all things. You can trust that he will restore *all* his children to his happiness and joy. In this moment, turn to him; lean on his tenderhearted mercy toward you, wherever you may need it. His endless, faithful mercies are always available to you, his beloved child.

PRAYER

Thank you, Father, for your tenderness and love toward me. I am grateful that your mercies never come to an end, and in heaven, you'll restore my losses and regrets into joy and innocence once again.

49

Alpha and Omega

"I am the Alpha and the Omega—the beginning and the end," says the Lord God. "I am the one who is, who always was, and who is still to come—the Almighty One. . . . I am the First and the Last. I am the living one. I died, but look—I am alive forever and ever!"

REVELATION 1:8, 17-18

People who have died and encountered heaven all seem to experience time outside of earth's one-dimensional linear framework, and they understand how it all fits together while they are there.

Gregg Rickert found himself in the presence of Jesus after a head-on car crash on a winding mountain road. Jesus took him to heaven where Gregg could "see" the nature of extra-dimensional time.

> When you're in front of God, you have absolute understanding. There's no questioning or reasoning; it's pure knowledge. . . . [Jesus] gestured to a four-foot portal to the side of him, like a round window, but it was like interdimensional time. We were outside of time and space.
>
> I was shown a timeline of two-dimensional time. I saw a beginning and end, but was outside of it. In heaven you're allowed to see through these portals, and I watched some kind of battle. It appeared to be in Egypt,

and two armies were going against each other with pyramids in the background—but I was watching it in reality. I was actually experiencing what was happening in their time.

What significance that moment had, I don't know, but I experienced it. I experienced it like watching a movie, but so much more real, even feeling what people were feeling or thinking. As I was watching that timeline at a point in time, I somehow knew that you were not allowed to go through that portal back into time, but I was allowed to see it. But when in heaven, you're experiencing it as it is actually happening.

I saw through another portal that an angel beckoned me to look through, and I was looking at a guy with blond hair, skinny guy, with a weird-looking haircut, and a girl. I said, "Oh, she's a pretty girl," and I saw this orb, this glowing one-foot round ball that was reverberating with excitement and energy, and I was told, "This is their child. . . ."

It was awesome. It was joy and excitement—just amazing.[150]

Miraculously, Gregg revived. Due to his injuries, he wasn't supposed to ever see, talk, walk, or run, but now he does it all. And one more twist was the confirmation Gregg received later of what he witnessed in heaven's multidimensional time.

So two-and-a-half years later, I meet this guy and this girl who were friends of our family, but I'd never met them [before this time]. They had a little blonde girl, about two-and-a-half years old, who looks up at me with so much excitement and joy. The mom said, "I

> don't know why she loves you so." And suddenly it hit me, this is the mom. This is the woman I saw with the skinny guy, and this must be the little unborn girl I saw in the portal.[151]

. . . .

God exists outside of all dimensions of time because he is the creator of time. He said, "I am the Alpha and the Omega, the First and the Last, the Beginning and the End" (Revelation 22:13, NIV). God said to Jeremiah, "Before I formed you in the womb I knew you" (Jeremiah 1:5, NIV). However, God can still experience one-dimensional time with his creation if he wishes. Jesus himself entered our one-dimensional time on earth and limited himself in order to relate to us.

In heaven, God experiences all time simultaneously. God is eternal. He sees all moments—the beginning, the end, and all points in between—in one eternal moment. This means God sees how everything will work out for good because he already is experiencing the past and future moments of earth, the final conquering of good over evil, the restoration of all things to their rightful places, and our future joy. God experiences the victory over all evil and suffering right now, even as you read this.

That's why we can trust his promises in Scripture. In the Sermon on the Mount, Jesus taught us not to worry about our lives—what we will eat, wear, or anything else. Instead, we should seek God's Kingdom and his will, and all these other things will be taken care of (see Matthew 6). He knows this is true because he already sees your future, so you can trust him with it.

Today, meditate on this truth about God. He is eternal. He alone knows the future, so he knows how the hardships you are currently facing are fitting into the victory he has already won for you. Find security in knowing that there will be redemption and restoration of all the trials and sufferings of this life, and heaven sees that now! So, in this moment and the ones to come, let God's promises bring you peace and comfort that God is in control, and everything will truly be okay.

PRAYER

Lord, how magnificent you are—the Beginning and the End. You know how difficult it is for me to not worry or be anxious about the future. Forgive me for not trusting you, the one who knows the future and has already won the victory. Today I will entrust what I cannot control into your hands, and I will seek your wisdom with what I can control.

50

Jesus, Our Advocate

My dear children, I am writing this to you so that you will not sin. But if anyone does sin, we have an advocate who pleads our case before the Father. He is Jesus Christ, the one who is truly righteous. He himself is the sacrifice that atones for our sins—and not only our sins but the sins of all the world.

1 JOHN 2:1-2

Alexa Hartung went into labor with her second child, but after the baby was delivered, Alexa looked down and saw she was bleeding profusely. During her near-death experience, she found herself in a heavenly courtroom undergoing a life review. In Alexa's life review, she saw how condemning accusations can't stand against the truth of God's grace, and that Jesus has the final word.

> During this Review, the Evil being was there. I looked at him; he was handsome, not ugly. Black hair, medium build, dressed in a brown robe with a black cord at his waist. His eyes caught my attention. They were a black void! There was no life or goodness in them. Intense in every way, his only Purpose was to possess, own, control my very Soul and make me suffer!! I shrank back in horror. Every time, during the Review that I erred or failed, he enjoyed it immensely.

He would shout out, "THERE! See how she messed up?" He would accuse me, "Why didn't she do better? Or help more? She ought to be punished!" I was desolate. My few, little good works didn't and couldn't measure up to God's perfect standard.

Then, when it was over, a huge deep voice boomed out: "IS SHE COVERED BY THE BLOOD OF THE LAMB?"

"YES!"

With that, Jesus looked at Satan and declared: "SHE'S MINE!"

The courtroom disappeared, and the evil being, Satan, screamed! He hissed like a snake, turned and whirled like a tornado, but got smaller and smaller. He shrunk down to a pile of dust and poof! He disappeared completely, after screaming in anger the whole time.

Everything in that setting was gone, except the heavenly crowd and Jesus Christ. He gazed at me with INCREDIBLE love! He held out his nail-pierced hands and wrists, that although healed completely, had the outline of the crucifixion marks. This was no wimpy Jesus. He was strong, powerful, tall as a ceiling, and shining all over! His long, white hair was nothing compared to his burning, liquid-gold eyes. They burned with Purity, Joy, and Purpose. He opened his mouth, and I heard a loud sound like a freight train! The rushing and roaring sound that came out was almost deafening. He spoke of who he was, and that he was my advocate with God the Father. I fell down in awe and worshiped him with my very Soul. I cried with Joy like a baby as I gazed up at his glorious, loving smile. He loved and accepted me—totally. I was filled with peace and contentment.[152]

....

Jesus is our advocate, and he alone can defend us against all of Satan's accusations. The word *Satan* literally means "accuser." Jesus never fell for Satan's accusations or temptations, and he alone was the sinless human who could take our place to offer a perfect sacrificial payment for our wrongdoings because he had no debts of his own (see 2 Corinthians 5:21). Now, Jesus represents our case and fights for us, declaring that our debts are paid in full by his blood and that no accusations against us will stand.

Remembering that Jesus is our advocate and defense against Satan's accusations can help us when we are feeling accused, condemned, or judged for something we've done. The apostle John tells us in 1 John 1:9, "If we confess our sins to him, he is faithful and just to forgive us our sins and to cleanse us from all wickedness." The Holy Spirit brings unconfessed sin to our minds so that we can confess and make it right between us and God and any other person we may have affected. Even though our sin has already been paid for and forgiven on the cross, admitting it to God turns us back to his leadership over our lives.

If you feel condemned for something you've already confessed to God and turned from, know that "there is no condemnation for those who belong to Christ Jesus" (Romans 8:1). If you hear shaming thoughts like, "You're terrible—look how you keep doing this" or "God's sick of you; he doesn't want anything to do with you anymore," know that these come from the accuser, not God. Jesus says, "You are my beloved," "You are mine," "You are forgiven," and "You are not condemned."

Today and every day, let Jesus protect you from these attacks of shame and condemnation and only listen to him. He's your defense attorney and advocate, and he's good at what he does—he wins every time!

PRAYER

Jesus, thank you for setting me free, not only from the debts I could not pay, but also from all accusations, shame, and condemnation aimed to drive me away from you. Show me if there's any unconfessed sin in my life, so I can admit it, turn back, and stay cleansed and connected to God. Thank you that nothing can separate me from you—my soul is safe in your salvation.

51

Worthy of Praise

Let the heavens be glad, and the earth rejoice!
Let the sea and everything in it shout his praise!
Let the fields and their crops burst out with joy!
Let the trees of the forest sing for joy
before the LORD, for he is coming!

PSALM 96:11-13

When Dean Braxton died of sepsis, he had the most amazing experience of witnessing all of creation praising God. Scripture talks about this, but it's hard to imagine here on earth. Dean describes praise as a beautiful, interactive love song from us to God and from God to us:

> God the Father was singing back to each and every being giving him praise before the throne. He was singing an individual love song to each of his creations. . . . There is an exchange of love words between God and each person. The only time I saw beings open their mouths was when they were singing praises to the Father at the throne. Every living being and creature praises the Father and Jesus. Every part of God's creation praises God all the time. To hear the flowers praise the Lord is wonderful. The birds sing praise to the Lord. Water praised the Lord. Mountains praised the Lord.[153]

Some people may consider it a metaphor when the psalmist declares, "The trees of the forest sing for joy . . . before the LORD" (Psalm 96:12-13, NIV). Yet many people who have had near-death experiences agree with Dean—creation does actually sing God's praise! When Heidi Barr died from a horseback riding accident, Jesus took her to the Father, and there she also experienced nature praising God with glorious melodies.

> I could see every single blade of grass. The most amazing part? The grass was singing! I will never ever forget what I saw and what I heard; what I witnessed. Each blade of grass was singing the praises of God. The music the grass made was astonishing, amazing, gorgeous, heavenly, awesome. The flowers and the trees were swaying in time to the song of the grass, and all were moving in the light of God. It was God's light flowing through everything, animating everything. As I watched this remarkable sight, I noticed a path through the meadow. I heard singing, people singing. They too were singing the praises of God.[154]

. . . .

Psalm 148 is a call for all of creation—including the sun, oceans, wind, trees, mountains, and living creatures—to praise God. Psalm 148:13 declares, "Let them all praise the name of the LORD. For his name is very great; his glory towers over the earth and heaven!" It's hard to fathom on earth, but people who have had NDEs consistently testify that in heaven, all creation really does praise God. Not because they must, or because God needs praise, but because his awe-inspiring, glorious presence *compels* it. Praise is a natural response when we truly encounter God's life-giving Spirit. Just as the crowd at a stadium erupts into shouts of praise at a last-second win, they don't do it because they must; they proclaim praise because they're participating in the glory of their team.

Giving God praise is our participation in his magnificent glory. When we praise him, we acknowledge his rightful place in our lives and our secure place under his protection and authority. Songs of praise can be directed at the greatness of God, and sometimes our worship can be the expression of our love or thanksgiving as we remember all he's done for us. And those with near-death experiences confirm the remarkable truth in Scripture, that God sings songs back to his children: "He will take delight in you with gladness. With his love, he will calm all your fears. *He will rejoice over you with joyful songs*" (Zephaniah 3:17, emphasis added).

It is inspiring to set our minds on God's majesty, sovereignty, faithfulness, love, and all the qualities that make him Almighty God who alone deserves our praise. All of creation praises him in heaven, and one day, all the earth will join in adoration and praise to our Creator, the only real source of life and love. Imagine how exhilarating it will be to join with the flowers and trees in singing praises to God!

Today, find time to focus your heart and worship God by singing praise to him. You could sing your favorite tune, listen and sing along to your favorite worship song, or write your own melody in praise to God. Picture yourself here on earth joining with all of heaven's chorus in gladness and adoration to God!

PRAYER

Heavenly Father, I praise you for your majesty and sovereignty in my life, and I praise you for all the beauty and blessings you have given me to enjoy. You alone are the source of life and every good thing, and I join with all of creation in proclaiming your mighty works and praising your name!

52

Holy and Pure

I saw the Lord, high and exalted, seated on a throne; and the train of his robe filled the temple. Above him were seraphim, each with six wings . . . calling to one another: "Holy, holy, holy is the LORD Almighty." . . . "Woe to me!" I cried. "I am ruined! For I am a man of unclean lips, and I live among a people of unclean lips, and my eyes have seen the King, the LORD Almighty."

ISAIAH 6:1-3, 5, NIV

Dr. Ron Smothermon was stabbed thirteen times by a man who had suffered a psychotic break. Suddenly time stopped. And there before Ron appeared what looked like a nuclear explosion of light and love. There was no doubt in his mind who this was: Almighty God.

> I can only compare him to a supernova made of *love*! No one could have imagined such a Person. He is so perfect, so awesome, yet even in his infinite power, he is pure, gentle, innocent, humble, and even modest. . . . Now I know the meaning of the word "Holy."[155] . . . I could see his purity. He is so pure and so innocent, so completely unlike me.[156]
>
> God is so pure, I could never think of myself as pure again—*not ever*. I understood in my bones that man[kind] is lost, and without the salvation of God

> we are forever lost. He is magnificent. There is nothing hidden about him. Everything you can see, hear, feel, or sense about him in any way is *pure*. I long to be like him, just a tiny slice of what he is. To have that tiny slice is worth your life, and it would be a bargain if you could make that deal. That is what recognized saints on Earth achieve—a tiny slice of God's purity.[157]

Ron felt the profound impact of God's holiness—perfect purity compared to our impurity. Ron said God's holiness came across as innocent, yet not naive—a stark contrast compared to our corrupted humanity. Ron said there was "nothing hidden about him," which is similar to how Dean Braxton also described God during his near-death experience:

> In heaven, I experienced "the fear of the Lord" [described] in Scripture. It is a sense of awe and respect. He's so pure—all these words don't seem right—so clean, nothing wrong, no evil, all so pure. It is holiness, but it's a "what you see is what you get" purity that is so wonderful. That's what I want to try to be: Holy—what you see is what you get.[158]

Susanne Seymoure was only twelve years old when she had a skiing accident that led to her NDE. Jesus and two angels took her to heaven, and after she experienced Jesus like a comfortable, loving dad, he told her, "I'm much more than you've seen so far." Here is what Susanne recalls:

> I watched in awe as this beautiful, beautiful light—all these points of golden light—kept coming up over the hills, coming together to form this enormous golden

> hand larger than the whole sky. It covered everything. The golden light was the ultimate of every great word, "The Almighty," "Sovereign," "All-Powerful," "Holy." I've since learned that all those words are meant to convey something, but that Something was more than all words can express . . . just, "Whoa!" . . . All that overwhelming glory and power are hard to connect with as a child, so he first came to me as a man, like a dad, but then he showed me that he was so holy, so mind-blowing in size and awe and grandeur—the ruler of the universe—nothing is greater.[159]

. . . .

God is *holy*. We've heard that before, but what does it actually mean? The Hebrew word translated "holy" is the word *kodesh*, which means "set apart for a purpose." The angels around God's throne cry out, "Holy, holy, holy is the Lord Almighty" because God is set apart, perfect, and unique from all he created. There is no one like God!

Those who have experienced clinical death and have been in the presence of God understand that what makes him holy and different is his incredible power and grandeur, blended with an innocence and purity that not even a child possesses. God has never once had an evil thought; however, God is not naive. Jesus fully experienced life's temptations and sufferings during his time on earth, yet he did not sin. God is pure. He has no evil thoughts, untrustworthy motives, or false judgments. Everything is out in the open because he is perfect in all his ways.

First Peter 1:15-16 tells us, "But just as he who called you is holy, so be holy in all you do; for it is written: 'Be holy, because I am holy'" (NIV). God knows you cannot be perfect until he perfects you in heaven one day. But you can live "set apart," holy unto God by offering yourself daily to do his will, mindful of being obedient to him as best you can. As Romans 6:19 says, "Just as you used to offer yourselves as slaves to impurity and to ever-increasing wickedness, so now offer yourselves as slaves to righteousness leading to holiness" (NIV).

Today, take time to focus on recognizing the purity and holiness of God, being grateful he lives in you and wants to lead and direct your life in his righteousness. Consider a commitment to live before God with greater purity, becoming more like a child who lives an innocent, open, honest life before him.

PRAYER

Holy God, I'm in awe of you. You are so different than I am—so pure, so innocent, so forthright, yet so mighty and powerful and all-knowing. It's impossible to imagine the totality of your greatness. You are holy! Help me to live a holy life; I offer my mind, body, and soul to you today, set apart to do your will.

53

Suffering Servant

He was despised and rejected by mankind, a man of suffering, and familiar with pain. . . . Surely he took up our pain and bore our suffering, yet we considered him punished by God, stricken by him, and afflicted. But he was pierced for our transgressions, he was crushed for our iniquities; the punishment that brought us peace was on him, and by his wounds we are healed.

ISAIAH 53:3-5, NIV

One of the most profound revelations of God is that he enters our suffering. When Jesus took the punishment for the sins of all humanity, God endured the depths of human suffering. But that was not the only time. He suffers with us still today.

Erica McKenzie experienced the suffering of God during her near-death experience. Though she believed in Jesus, she had struggled for years with an eating disorder and a diet pill addiction that eventually caused her heart to stop. At first, Erica found herself in God's presence. Flooded with unconditional love, she felt ecstatic joy that she was God's beloved child. Later, as Erica and God looked down together on planet Earth, Erica felt something shift dramatically.

> Then all of a sudden, I feel this feeling I haven't felt this whole time with God in all of these lessons. I feel this tremendous amount of sadness, and at first,

> I didn't know where it was coming from. I knew it wasn't coming from me, and then as soon as I had that realization, it felt almost as if you were a parent and you lost all your children at once, they all perished. . . . That's what it felt like to me. It was so powerful, and then I understood it was coming from God—that feeling of sadness. And I remember looking at God and saying, "God, why are you sad?"
>
> I looked . . . and the whole entire planet was engulfed in flames. And then I started panicking, almost like I can't breathe, because I know my family is down there. My children are down there. . . . [Then] I see this silver luminescent life force . . . and they were lifting off, unscathed, in between the flames and coming towards God, . . . and they were souls. They were souls connected to God. And it was this huge relief to me . . . but then again, I feel an even more tremendous sadness from God. Almost unbearable. And I asked God, "No, no, God—why are you sad, look! They're all coming to Heaven. They're coming home." And God said to me, "Erica, hand in hand with the gift of life, I give free will." . . . His sadness was for the ones that were left behind. And I looked again, and I could see that some of the souls weren't lifting off. . . . Free will means God doesn't make the choice for us; God gives us the gift to make that choice if we want to have that love connection with our Creator or not.[160]

When Randy Kay's body shut down from a pulmonary embolism, he found himself walking in heaven with Jesus. He experienced the joy and the sadness God feels intertwined with the people he loves. In Randy's life review, Jesus replayed for

Randy a time when, even as a believer in Christ, Randy and his friends became enamored with repeatedly visiting a "haunted house."

> Now I was standing in a cornfield across from the house on Blood Point Road, as a crying sound like that of a lost child, blew through the wind. Behind me I could see the gothic house with its vacant windows. . . .
>
> "You opened the doorway to mine enemy, beloved, and you were entertained by the spirit of darkness," [Jesus explained].
>
> "That child I heard in the cornfield—was the voice really a demon?"
>
> "Yes, and each of the bizarre manifestations you saw. Did you expect anything else?"
>
> "I was ignoring you," I said. "No, I knew better, but I assumed that you weren't watching me." . . .
>
> "My Spirit lived within you, my beloved, so of course, I always knew what you were doing. You grieved me, beloved."
>
> "Forgive me."
>
> "I already did," he said.
>
> "And why are you showing this to me, Lord?"
>
> I suddenly remembered repenting of my indiscretions, . . . but I felt something else. It was as if I had caused Jesus to sacrifice himself all over again for me—as if I was reopening the wounds of his persecution. . . .
>
> "Sin, beloved, is a rejection of me. The unbeliever never knew me, but my children know my voice, and when they sin, they refuse my voice." . . .

> "And that opened me to hearing the voice of the demons? I rejected you all over again."
>
> "Yes, beloved, you ignored me. When I became your Lord, I breathed life into your spirit so that we could dwell with each other. When you sinned, you were like a runaway child, but when you repented, you came home to me."
>
> Strangely, I felt no condemnation from Jesus in seeing my sins. Rather, I felt even more thankful for his grace. He knew my heart, and he knew that I wanted to return home.[161]

Even as God is saddened by our rebellious choices, the opposite is also true—our good actions can cause God tremendous delight and joy. In his life review, Jesus showed Howard Storm a time when his sister was grieving the loss of a pet. Howard got out of bed, went into her room, and held her—comforting her. "Jesus and the angels were so filled with joy that I had been willing to do that," Howard said, watching back his act of kindness.[162]

....

Jesus came to earth as our Suffering Servant. He descended from heaven to humbly love and serve humanity, yet he suffered at our hands. He was crucified to atone for the punishment of our sins, and his blood purchased healing and forgiveness for our souls.

God still suffers when unbelievers reject his love and the relentless ways he seeks to draw them near to himself. But he also grieves when believers continually reject his guiding voice and rebel against him, pretending he doesn't see their thoughts and actions. We take God's grace for granted when we assume that forgiveness justifies willful rebellion, telling ourselves that sin is no big deal. To God, this feels like rejection, and our actions can grieve him deeply. Scripture says, "Do not grieve the Holy Spirit of God. . . . Get rid of all bitterness, rage and anger, brawling and slander, along with every form of malice" (Ephesians 4:30-31, NIV).

We need to honor and treasure the sufferings of Jesus and be grateful and humble, knowing he suffered in our place. We should genuinely never want to grieve his heart again. Yet even still, God never withdraws his love, and he doesn't condemn us even when we grieve him. However, we must realize that our actions can either cause God's heart to suffer and bring negative consequences to our lives, or they can bring him great joy and lead us into his abundant life—the choice is ours. Today, commit to bringing joy to the heart of God in how you live.

PRAYER

Lord, that you suffered to pay for all my sins is such an astounding demonstration of your great love for me. Forgive me when I take your grace for granted, ignoring your voice and going my own stubborn way. I want to bring you joy, not sorrow, through my actions as I walk with you today. Thank you for your unfailing love and forgiveness that lets me start each day new.

54

Calls Us to Forgive

Pray like this: Our Father in heaven, may your name be kept holy. May your Kingdom come soon. May your will be done on earth, as it is in heaven. Give us today the food we need, and forgive us our sins, as we have forgiven those who sin against us. And don't let us yield to temptation, but rescue us from the evil one.

MATTHEW 6:9-13

As gospel recording artist Tony Davis rounded the corner to pick up his wife in downtown Los Angeles, shots rang out, and he heard bullets striking his car. Little did he know that he had driven into a gang initiation, poised to kill a man as a rite of passage. They shot Tony five times, leaving him to die. As his soul floated up toward the clouds, a window opened through which he saw the glorious city of God. Love, peace, and joy filled his heart, and the cares of this world disappeared. As he anticipated going through the window, God said, "It's not yet your time."

"No, no, no, God. I don't want to go back to that world and those hard-hearted people," Tony pleaded. God replied, "There's a message I need you to deliver to my people. A message of forgiveness, and triumph over tragedy." Tony continued to beg God to let him stay, and again he heard, "Tony, I need you to deliver this message to my people."

Tony found himself back in his body, in a hospital after being dead for thirty minutes. An emergency tracheotomy had cut his vocal cords, so Tony was back, but he would never sing again. After seeing his miraculous resuscitation, the doctors rushed to amputate his leg where the gang had shot his femoral artery. As Tony lay there waiting to lose his leg, he started talking to God.

Tony felt a warm, loving Presence enter the room, and he heard one word, "Forgive." Tony lay there wrestling with this command. *You've got to be kidding, look what they did to me, God. I never shot anybody. I've never held a gun, and these guys, for no reason—they shot me!*

"If you forgive, I'll make you whole," God's voice spoke into his spirit. As he struggled with what God was asking, Tony realized that forgiveness is not a feeling; it's a choice. *All right, God, I forgive. I give it all to you.* A warmth came up through his leg and right up to his throat. Today, Tony not only walks on two legs, but he sings God's praises as he teaches us all to forgive.[163]

Douglas had led a life of crime, which made him both rich and famous. But Douglas discovered none of that mattered when his car skidded into a parked semitruck on the side of the highway, and he died. In his near-death experience, he saw his name in the Book of Life from when he had accepted Jesus as a child, but he also saw the book of his deeds that were not pleasing to God. When he resuscitated, he changed his ways and started following Jesus. However, Douglas discovered that following God's will was not always easy, even after experiencing heaven. Life was a struggle for Douglas, just as it is for all of us. For Douglas, his thoughts were dominated by anger and a desire for revenge against those who had betrayed him.

> I was trying desperately to change who I was and what I had become, but as hard as I would try, I could not escape myself. . . . My hope of forgiving others for what they [had] done to me was another impossibility

> and the word *forgiveness* would get stuck in my throat when trying to recite the Lord's Prayer. I couldn't even finish the prayer. My "walk" towards God had hit a roadblock. . . . I began to pray to God asking him for help in becoming able to forgive those people who had wronged me. . . . What God did show me was that even though I myself (the old man) never would forgive, Jesus Christ existed in me as a new person and had done all the forgiving that has ever needed to be done. However, he was also telling me that I had to allow him to become me.[164]

. . . .

God is a forgiver. He declared his name to Moses saying, "The LORD, the LORD, the compassionate and gracious God, slow to anger, abounding in love and faithfulness, maintaining love to thousands, and forgiving wickedness, rebellion and sin. Yet he does not leave the guilty unpunished" (Exodus 34:6-7, NIV). While God will always forgive, he is also just, so we can trust him to help us when we need to forgive. He does not ignore the wrong that we and others do; he takes it upon himself. God forgave us for every wrong when Jesus died on the cross, and he expects us to forgive others. We can ask God to give us his power to forgive when it's difficult.

Forgiveness may feel hard to do because we can't always control our feelings, but as Jesus instructs, forgiveness is a choice. It involves giving to God the hurt, the pain, the shame of what happened, as well as the feeling that "we did not deserve this" and are justified in punishing that other person by not letting them off the hook. God knows that we are actually keeping ourselves hooked to the pain and hurt of the past when we nurse these feelings. We are the ones chained to the past wrongs, not those who hurt us. God wants us free.

God promises that he will be just and that we can trust him with all justice. Those that have harmed us will be handled by God in the way that he knows is best. That means we don't have to worry about fairness, or what we deserve, or whether others ever acknowledge what they've done or not. God will take care of all of that. He has not treated us as our wrongdoings deserve—he has freely forgiven us. In return, he asks us to do the same for others.

There may be harms done to you that seem far too difficult to forgive. In those cases, visualize placing these hurts at the foot of the cross and picture the blood of Jesus covering them. Jesus suffered the payment for the sins of others, too, so you both can be free.

Is there someone you need to forgive? Sometimes unforgiveness hides behind avoidance and a desire to not have to face what may be painful. God is with you to help you forgive from your heart. Today, ask God to show you any unforgiveness you need to release and let his blood cover it once and for all. You can trust that he will take care of the rest.

PRAYER

Dear God, search my heart. Show me if there is any resentment, bitterness, or unforgiveness in me. I choose to trust you to be just, and so I will put justice back in your hands. I forgive [fill in the blank] for what they did to me, and I release the need to punish into your hands. I forgive as you have forgiven me.

55

Living Light

You have rescued me from death; you have kept my feet from slipping.
So now I can walk in your presence, O God, in your life-giving light.

PSALM 56:13

Saul of Tarsus, a Pharisee, was on his way to Damascus, intending to persecute Christians there, when he experienced the same piercing light of God that those with near-death experiences describe. This brilliant light was so intensely alive that it dropped him to his knees.

> As I was on the road, approaching Damascus about noon, a very bright light from heaven suddenly shone down around me. I fell to the ground and heard a voice saying to me, "Saul, Saul, why are you persecuting me?"
>
> "Who are you, lord?" I asked.
>
> And the voice replied, "I am Jesus the Nazarene, the one you are persecuting." The people with me saw the light but didn't understand the voice speaking to me.
>
> I asked, "What should I do, Lord?"
>
> And the Lord told me, "Get up and go into Damascus, and there you will be told everything you are to do."

> I was blinded by the intense light and had to be led by the hand to Damascus by my companions. A man named Ananias lived there. He was a godly man, deeply devoted to the law, and well regarded by all the Jews of Damascus. He came and stood beside me and said, "Brother Saul, regain your sight." And that very moment I could see him!
>
> Then he told me, "The God of our ancestors has chosen you to know his will and to see the Righteous One and hear him speak. For you are to be his witness, telling everyone what you have seen and heard. What are you waiting for? Get up and be baptized. Have your sins washed away by calling on the name of the Lord."[165]

After his conversion, Saul went by the name Paul. He was so affected by this experience that he became a missionary, spreading the message of Jesus to different parts of the world on his journeys. The apostle Paul wrote many of the New Testament letters.

Most people who encounter God or Jesus in their NDEs describe a brilliant, dazzling light, alive and full of energy, impossible to describe in human language. Dean Braxton was dead for an hour and forty-five minutes after his organs shut down. Cedric Pisegna had an NDE in his sleep. Both men share their own descriptions of this divine light during their encounters. Here is what Dean describes:

> Jesus is pure light! His brightness was before me, around me, part of me, and in me. He is brighter than the noonday sun, but we can still look at him in Heaven. . . . Jesus is more beautiful, wonderful, and glorious than I can explain. . . . I looked into his face.

> How do I tell you what his face looks like? His face was as if it were liquid crystal glass made up of pure love, light, and life.[166]

Cedric also describes his experience with the divine light:

> I was standing before the throne of God! I was experiencing the pleasure all humans seek all our lives, the joy for which we were made. God's presence is the ultimate pleasure for which we long. . . . What I encountered when I stood before God was glorious and electric. I wasn't allowed to see a form, but what I did see was light. It was as if I were looking at the sun with my eyes closed, yet even more luminescent. Psalm 104:1-2 tells us the truth that "God is clothed with honor and majesty, and covers himself with light as with a garment." I didn't just see the light, the brightness embraced me. The light was somehow alive. In addition to the brightness, there was an overwhelming glory. . . . God's glory is not just something I observed, it was an electricity and ecstasy that I felt. It was a rhythmic powerful surge that ran all through me.[167]

Dean and Cedric both continued to follow the Light they experienced after they came back. And just like Paul, as Jesus illuminated their steps one by one, they both found a new mission in life. Dean became a pastor who shares God's love in schools and prisons, and Cedric became a Passionist priest, focused on helping people live in the saving grace of the cross.

. . . .

The living light of God is a beautiful mystery that goes beyond our earthly understanding. We know that God is love, so we can trust that his ways are good. His light embodies all of love's qualities as it shines upon us and in us, illuminating the path we should follow. The apostle Paul encountered Jesus in a powerful, brilliant light and knew this light held authority. Paul responded to the simple instructions Jesus gave him regarding the steps he should take and the course-corrections he needed to make moving forward. We, too, can experience God's guidance and clarity when we turn to him.

Have you ever felt lost in the darkness of this broken world? It can be overwhelming and confusing, like you don't know where to turn or what to do. But there is hope. Jesus said, "I have come as a light to shine in this dark world, so that all who put their trust in me will no longer remain in the dark" (John 12:46).

Jesus is our light, filling us inside as well as shining a path before us, so we don't have to walk in darkness. Just like an oil lamp carried at night, the light of Jesus often reveals only a few steps at a time. As you trust in his light and follow where he leads, the darkness and ambiguity will disappear step by step, and you'll find the clarity and strength to keep moving forward. So don't give up hope. Let the Light of life guide you; you can trust him.

Take a moment today and focus on allowing the living light of God to fill you, and as you do, surrender to follow his path. As he illuminates each step, walk out in his light and respond to his guidance and leadership. As you continue to do this, watch how his light will not only illuminate your path ahead, but also powerfully radiate through you—blessing your family, friendships, community, and world.

PRAYER

Dear God, thank you for the gift of your active, powerful, guiding light in my life. Help me to surrender to your guidance and will every moment of every day, following the path you've illuminated before me step by step. I want to radiate the light of your presence, Lord, with everything I am.

Honest Relationship

So I say, walk by the Spirit, and you will not gratify the desires of the flesh. For the flesh desires what is contrary to the Spirit, and the Spirit what is contrary to the flesh. . . . But the fruit of the Spirit is love, joy, peace, forbearance, kindness, goodness, faithfulness, gentleness and self-control. Against such things there is no law.

GALATIANS 5:16-17, 22-23, NIV

The day Santosh Acharjee's pancreas ruptured and his heart stopped beating, he found himself standing before someone he knew without a doubt was Almighty God. "I didn't know who He was except that He was God," Santosh recalls.[168] He saw a very narrow gate into the Kingdom of Heaven that was open to him, and he asked the Lord how he could go through that narrow gate when he returned.

> "I want an honest relationship," was his reply. "I want to see how true, how sincere, how honest you are with me, not just once a week, but every day, 365 days a year. How honest are you—that's the relationship I want."
>
> I sincerely didn't understand, so I said, "Lord, I'm a simple man, please tell me what I must do so that next time you see me, I can walk through that door."
>
> He gave me one directive and five instructions. [The] first directive was, "Love your family, and love

your children." That was mandatory; "You must love your family and love your children." Then the first instruction was, "Always tell the truth." Always tell the truth has two meanings for me. First, don't lie. But second, tell the truth about what you are witnessing here in front, God's reality and the narrow door, and what you are seeing on your left, this abyss of darkness and lake of fire. And I knew he wanted me to share the truth with anyone about what he was showing me. [The] second instruction was, "The wages of sin is death; from this day forward commit no more sins." [In the] third instruction he said, "Surrender yourself completely—I should underline completely—in your daily life." [The] fourth instruction [was], "Walk with me." I did not understand what that meant, "Walk with me." I came from a different background; it made no sense. But I now realize he meant if he's going forward and I'm going backward or sideways, we're not walking together. And the fifth instruction, "Always be kind to the poor; be generous to the poor. They need your help." We most often think of financial help only, but people can be poor in many ways. They can be physically poor, spiritually poor, emotionally poor, as well as financially poor. . . .

The Lord said, "Do not be afraid. I will be with you, and I will guide you."[169]

. . . .

Santosh did not understand what it meant to walk with God, but he later learned after reading the Bible that God's Spirit is in every believer and will guide us on our journey in life. This is what walking with God is all about. An honest relationship with us is what God wants most, and not just at church on Sundays, but all day, every day.

This is really the secret to spiritual growth—walking daily in a surrendered posture saying, "Not my will be done, but what's *your* will in this situation, Lord?" We must stay honest with God, talking over everything throughout our day: "What do you want me to say to this person, Lord?" "I shouldn't be thinking this, should I, Jesus?"

Walking by the Spirit means we go through the day in a continual, honest conversation, confessing sinful thoughts or actions that sneak in, and asking the Spirit to teach us and help us grow in obedience to him. We don't have to try hard to stop doing bad things or try hard to see good things grow—when we stay in connection with God, this will happen naturally.

As you walk with God in honest conversation, listen for his prompting in your spirit and be willing to follow his Spirit's lead. He will guide you into a life of purpose and joy, including loving others, serving those in need, and being a peacemaker. And just as Galatians 5 says, you'll see sinful, negative patterns retreat and experience a natural increase of the fruit of God's Spirit: "love, joy, peace, patience, kindness, goodness, faithfulness, gentleness, and self-control" (verses 22-23). Imagine how fulfilling your life will be with these fruits blossoming and growing within you!

Take some time today to reflect on your relationship with God. Ask yourself if you are relating to God in an honest, genuine way. Try to identify which fruits of the Spirit are healthy in you and which ones need extra attention and care to fully reflect God to the world around you. Then, it's really simple—stay connected! Walk with God's Spirit in honest, transparent conversation and be willing to do what he prompts you to do, and you'll grow to become all God created you to be.

PRAYER

Holy Spirit of God, thank you for living in me to guide me and do life with me. I'm amazed that you want a genuine and honest relationship with me, and I want to live that way daily with you. Thank you for your promise that as I walk with you, willing to obey your promptings, you will produce good fruit in me to bless my life and those around me.

57

Our Great Encourager

May the God who gives endurance and encouragement give you the same attitude of mind toward each other that Christ Jesus had, so that with one mind and one voice you may glorify the God and Father of our Lord Jesus Christ.

ROMANS 15:5-6, NIV

As the ambulance rushed fourteen-year-old Sarah from the car accident to the hospital, her life played before her, and Sarah thought she was going to die. She realized what a tragic, short life she had lived, growing up abused and under constant blame and verbal aggression. Then Sarah had a near-death experience in which she brought her toughest questions to Jesus, and he encouraged her heart.

Why wouldn't God protect me from being abused? Didn't I love him enough, that he might help me like the people in the Bible? She started to hear answers back to her thoughts. The voice, tender and soothing, was offering her healing replies. Feeling reassured, Sarah asked more questions.

"Why won't God protect me?"

The voice replied, "He will."

"Why won't God stick up for me?"

The voice explained, in a comforting way, that all these things were only temporary. With each reply, this abused young teenager felt the crippling, crushing weight she had carried release from her spirit. She felt safe for the first time in her life.

She opened up to him about the things she had been accused of that she had not done, and the pain she felt when nobody believed her.

"I believe you," he said.

She began going through the rest of her thoughts in the freedom of his comfort and safety.

"I wish I were beautiful."

"You are," he said reassuringly.

With each answer, Sarah felt joy filling her spirit until she thought she would burst.

"I wish I was perfect."

As someone who had suffered abuse for not measuring up, Sarah always thought perfection was the only way to be accepted and loved. She feared God would be mad at her, too, because she wasn't perfect.

She heard, "You are. . . . There is nothing you could do that could ever change the way God feels about you. . . . God loves [you]."

"He does?" she asked, astonished.

"Yes, he does," the voice said gently.

"I wish I was special, like the people in the Bible."

"You are."

"Really? I am?" Sarah couldn't imagine holding so much value to anyone, and each reassuring reply was healing her wounded soul.

"Yes, you are," he said.

Sarah shared that every molecule in her body was "bursting with LOVE and BLISS" from the overwhelming joy she was feeling. Then she suddenly exclaimed, "I just want to be with God. I just want to be with you!" As she turned around, what she saw took her breath away:

> There before me was the most BEAUTIFUL man I have ever seen in my whole life! . . . His eyes were wide with excitement and overflowing with LOVE and JOY. . . . There is no living person to ever exist that could match the BEAUTY of Jesus Christ. He was perfect in every sense of the word. He ran to me, and me to him. He embraced me and held me so close.[170]

. . . .

God is a masterful encourager. Our English word *encourage* means to infuse with courage or put courage in a person. God, by his Holy Spirit, does exactly this when he speaks words of value, worth, love, and assurance into our hearts and minds.

We tend to hear only the negative, critical voices of discouragement—demanding, demeaning voices that crowd our thoughts and cause us to feel abandoned and isolated. Yet God views each one of us as a beautiful masterpiece. He always sees our positive potential, even when he needs to discipline us. Though it can be difficult, we must resist the lies from the evil one, who is constantly at work attempting to steal our true identities in Christ.

When our heads are filled with negative, discouraging words instead of uplifting and hopeful ones, we will not have encouragement to give to others, since we cannot give what we don't have. This is part of the deceit of sin and evil. It beats us down in our minds so that we harden our hearts toward God and others, restricting his uplifting presence and power in our lives. In the Bible, God tells us to "encourage one another daily . . . so that none of [us] may be hardened by sin's deceitfulness" (Hebrews 3:13, NIV).

Today, take some focused time to listen and receive the

encouraging words God is speaking over your life: *You are worth more than you can imagine to God* (see Matthew 6:26). *You are his beloved, unique child* (see 1 John 3:1). *You have a special calling and purpose only he knows* (see Jeremiah 1:5). *You are his beautiful masterpiece* (see Ephesians 2:10). Meditate on these truths from Scripture and let God's words of blessing sink deep into your heart and mind. Then, ask God how you can be his voice of encouragement to another person today.

PRAYER

Lord, thank you for your encouragement. Help me to listen for your Holy Spirit's voice—the voice that speaks the truth. I reject the deceitful lie that you are the voice that shames, demeans, or is never happy with me, and I will believe only what you say about me. Help me to encourage others in the same way.

58

Light of the World

Jesus spoke to the people once more and said,
"I am the light of the world. If you follow me, you won't have to walk
in darkness, because you will have the light that leads to life."
JOHN 8:12

Jim Woodford's first sincere prayer came the moment he knew he was dying. "God, forgive me!" he cried out, in a moment of spiritual clarity, as he collapsed on the steering wheel of his parked truck. He found himself in the presence of three angels of regal stature and beauty. One was ten feet tall, which he discovered was his guardian, another twelve feet tall, which was a scribe recording his life, and the third, a fifteen-foot-tall warrior angel. Jim was in awe.

> Then they all lined up in front of me with the tallest angel in the center. He was a warrior angel, dressed as a warrior—he was clearly in charge. . . . But what astounded me, is the three bowed to me. A bow of reverence, of deep respect, and it lasted a long time. I said, "Why do you bow to me, I'm only a man. As unworthy as I am, I should bow to you." "James," the Guardian said, "when we look at mankind, we see the light of our Master in each of you." It's one of the most beautiful things I remember—that God's light was still

> in me—they could see it, despite all my failures. It's in there no matter what we've done, but it's up to us to let his light shine out.[171]

Later in his near-death experience, Jim saw the source of this light—the Light of the world.

> I turned to look for the warrior angel, and twenty feet away on a hillside is the tall angel bent very low on one knee, holding up his hands with a small book in front of another figure I had never seen before. And as magnificent as the angels were, this figure outshined the angels, and not just that the colors were different but a grandeur and majesty. . . . He was reading whatever the Guardian was holding up.
>
> And I started to make my way over there because there was a golden light flowing off the person, and it flowed like water from the top down the hillside slope. And I noticed as the slow-moving liquid light flowed over the flowers, they grew even more beautiful. The light made its way down toward me, and as it encircled my feet, I was filled with this incredible knowledge that I was looking at Jesus Christ, the Son of God. . . . I felt so ashamed because this little slim book the Guardian held in his hands, no thicker than a little roadside [diner] menu, was the book of my life [my deeds done for God]. Then the images came out of the book and began to replay as they enlarged and passed overhead. . . . I began to cry as I was so ashamed, and realized had I lived my life as I should have, my book would not be [the size of] a little cheap roadside menu. I'm determined Jesus is going to need a forklift to lift

> my book next time! I didn't deserve it, but I was given a second chance.

Since returning from his NDE, Jim has traveled the world telling people about Jesus, the Light of the world. Jim is determined to let his light shine and bring glory to God through his life.

> I physically see the light of God in people now—if I concentrate, I see it. I think when you go through the veil of death and come back, you're given certain gifts, . . . [and] I physically see the goodness and the light of God in people.
>
> When we talk about the image of God, it's the image of his Light. That's why I travel the world reminding people, it's the light of God in you that matters. And life is hard. Dying is easy. Relationships fail, financial difficulty, disappointments—life is hard. And so that light becomes dim. . . . But God stands ready to rekindle that candle of light within you. It is *his* light.[172]

....

Jesus is the Light of the world. He brings his light of hope, healing, love, and life to people struggling in darkness. And *you* are also the light of the world (see Matthew 5:14). Both are true! He wants his light in you to shine on others.

We are merely instruments of his love and light at work in the world. As Paul encouraged believers, "We now have this light shining in our hearts, but we ourselves are like fragile clay jars containing this great treasure. This makes it clear that our great power is from God, not from ourselves" (2 Corinthians 4:7). Our strength to make a difference in the world comes from God's light in us. God's light is in you for a purpose, and he wants to bring his light to the spiritually dark places of our world through you. We would never light a lamp or a candle and then hide it in a dark box. Instead, we place the candle where it can bring the greatest light to the darkness (see Matthew 5:15-16).

Take some time today to reflect on the light within you and how you can radiate it to others in your life. It may be that your neighbor is isolated or struggling with depression, and God wants you to bring his light of hope to her. Or perhaps a friend is feeling overwhelmed by the challenges of work, parenting, or marriage, and you can shine God's peace upon him and his situation, illuminating a way forward. In gratitude for the light within you, respond to opportunities he gives you to radiate his light onto others. When you do this, your good deeds are glorifying God. Today, commit to being willing to shine God's light to everyone he brings in your path.

PRAYER

Dear God, thank you for shining your light in the darkness, shining your light upon my life, and bringing hope to a world in need of you. Help me to radiate your love and light to everyone you put in my path.

59

Sacrificial Love

Dear friends, let us love one another, for love comes from God. Everyone who loves has been born of God and knows God. Whoever does not love does not know God, because God is love. This is how God showed his love among us: He sent his one and only Son into the world that we might live through him. This is love: not that we loved God, but that he loved us and sent his Son as an atoning sacrifice for our sins. Dear friends, since God so loved us, we also ought to love one another.

1 JOHN 4:7-11, NIV

As Dean Braxton encountered heaven's splendor during his near-death experience, he found himself in the presence of Jesus. Dean remembers being especially aware of Jesus' feet, and the sacrificial love he felt coming from them was something he would never forget. The impact it had on Dean led him to give up his career as a corrections officer to travel the world, sharing the love of Jesus with every person possible.

> When I got on the other side of the forest, that's when I saw Jesus Christ. He was really bright, brighter than any light I've ever seen, even the sun. . . . I looked at his feet, and when I looked at his feet, I saw the holes—not in the feet but the ankles, in the talocrural joint. . . . I remember thinking to myself, *His feet love me.* It was like I was literally receiving the fullness

> of the love of God through the feet of Jesus. Then I started looking up and every portion of him was loving me. His entire being loved me.[173]

Richard Sigmund, whose NDE followed a terrible car accident, also saw the nail holes in Jesus' resurrected body—an eternal reminder to all of heaven of the sacrificial love of God.

> Then Jesus walked toward me. He stopped a few feet from me, and I fell on my face like a dead man. I remember looking at the nail holes through his feet. They shone with a light from the inside of beautiful, beautiful Jesus. He suffered this for me! I had no words. He touched me, and I was able to stand. I did not feel worthy to stand or look at his face. He reached out his fingers, lifted my chin and said, "Son, look at me. I love you. Even though you have been disobedient and haven't done what I have told you to do, I still love you, and I desire for you to tell my people the glorious things that my Father has made for them." He took my hand and began to walk with me like a father would a little child. We walked a little farther and he said, "Tell my people I am coming soon. And I love them." Then he gave me a big hug and kissed me on the cheek and said, "I love you, too." He held out his hands in front of me, and I saw where the nails pierced him. The wounds were open, and yet shining through them was a beautiful light.[174]

....

The fullness of God's love is far too great to express adequately in words, for it is supernatural, unconditional, and far more exhilarating than anything we could ever experience here on earth. God's love is more than just a feeling; it involves sacrificing oneself for the good of another. The Scriptures remind us that the clearest picture of God's love is what Jesus did on the cross when he died to pay for the sins of every person.

Jesus said, "This is my commandment: Love each other in the same way I have loved you. There is no greater love than to lay down one's life for one's friends" (John 15:12-13). God's love is sacrificial. You can try to understand it as you think of those you'd do anything to protect. But even that love doesn't compare to the all-encompassing, incomprehensible love that allowed your sin and mine to nail Jesus—Love himself—to a cross.

The nail-scarred hands and feet of Jesus eternally show God's relentless, saving love toward you and every person he created. God's definition of love includes the willingness to sacrifice life, yet we can also follow his example in smaller, daily ways. Will you lay down your time for the good of another? Will you lay down your right to win an argument for the sake of love? Will you lay down your pride when you need to apologize and reconcile? Perhaps you need to lay down what you're "owed" or "deserve" to love someone else like God does. Right now, begin asking God to show you ways to love others with the same sacrificial love he demonstrated for you.

PRAYER

Dear God, thank you for unconditionally, sacrificially loving me when I do not deserve it. Help me contemplate the breadth and depth of your sacrificial love for me today. Show me ways to lay down my life as a sacrifice of love back to you.

60

God of the Ripple Effect

The one who plants and the one who waters have one purpose, and they will each be rewarded according to their own labor. For we are co-workers in God's service.

1 CORINTHIANS 3:8-9, NIV

God loves to empower his children as vessels to accomplish his purposes in the world. Many who have near-death experiences come back talking about the emphasis God makes on the importance of our words and actions, and the ripple effect each word and action has on humanity. The following are accounts of four women, each of whom clinically died and gained a profound understanding of this while in the presence of God.

> **Erica:** Resting in [God's] palm was a massive rock. . . . At once, God let loose the rock and together we watched it fall. . . . I saw a vast body of water appear. It was greater than the largest ocean and into the water the rock plunged. Together, we watched as a single ripple of water appeared. God said, "Mankind is the water. You are the ripple." I watched the single ripple expand until I could no longer see it. I repeated, "I am the ripple." And then God turned to me and said, "Like the ripple affects the water, so too do man's words and actions affect mankind." . . . I began to comprehend its significance.

Every word, thought, and action, no matter how small, affected everyone and everything. I had no idea of the power and consequences of my thoughts, my words, and actions.[175]

Penny: First, he showed me the good. The things that I had done that I felt really good about did not come up. But the things that came up were like a scene in the grocery store that I had forgotten about. There was a woman in line in front of me, and she was short just a couple of dollars. She was trying to figure out what to put back, . . . and I said, "It's okay, it's okay—I've got it." And I gave her the money. And so, I'm seeing this scene like I'm there, and immediately it flashes forward, and I see this [same] woman working in a food pantry. She's blessing these people with food. And God said, "I want you to see the ripple effect of every little act of kindness."[176]

Alexa: I saw how my acting, or not acting, rippled in effect toward other people and their lives. It wasn't until then that I understood how each little decision or choice affects the world.[177]

Mary: My life was laid bare for all its good and bad. And one of the things we did was look at many, many, many events throughout my life that I would've otherwise called terrible or horrible or sad or bad or tragic. And instead of looking at an event in isolation or looking at how it impacted me and my little world, I had the most remarkable experience of seeing the ripple effects of the event when seen twenty-five, thirty, thirty-five times removed. . . . And looking at how an

> event that I would have said was bad, changed me and changed others such that again and again and again, I was shown that indeed it's true that beauty comes of all things. It was really a life-changing experience.[178]

....

It is amazing to realize how God allows us to influence the entire world through the choices we make. God could do it all himself, but his very nature is to empower us to work together with him as his coworkers. Every word we speak and every action we take makes a difference—for good or for bad. So we must be mindful and careful to live according to God's will and ways. When we do this, God works through us to bring his Kingdom to earth, displacing evil in the world with his goodness and love.

Every act of love and kindness matters, and every encouraging word matters, so we must decide each day if we will bless with our words and actions, or if we won't. We have a choice to make with each interaction we encounter along our life's path. As Deuteronomy 30:19 says, "Today I have given you the choice between life and death, between blessings and curses. Now I call on heaven and earth to witness the choice you make. Oh, that you would choose life, so that you and your descendants might live!"

It is interesting to note that there is no in-between. We either end up blessing the world through the ripple effect of positive words and deeds, or doing the opposite through our negative words and deeds. Thankfully, we know that God can bring good out of any situation. No matter what, he can take the negative and use it in positive ways for our good and the good of all humanity, for he alone can make beauty out of ashes. But he gives us the rewarding opportunity to partner with him in making a positive difference in the world.

With God, you can have a much greater influence on humanity than you could ever imagine having alone. Today, think of ways you can partner with God to bless the world through your words and actions, regardless of how insignificant they may seem. One day, you may witness the incredible impact that your faithfulness has had on millions of lives!

PRAYER

Dear God, thank you for trusting me and empowering me to partner with you to make a positive difference in the world. Help me to be a blessing in all I say and do, knowing that even the smallest interactions done in love have great ripple effects on all of humanity.

FAQs on NDEs

From *Imagine the God of Heaven Study Guide*

1. **What is a near-death experience (NDE)?**

   A near-death experience can occur during clinical death, which is when the heart stops beating and all brain functions cease. When the person is resuscitated, they claim to have been conscious somewhere beyond their physical body, experiencing the life to come. These are referred to as "*near-death* experiences" because the person came back to life. Although such experiences have also been reported in cases without proof of clinical death, the stories in *Imagine the God of Heaven* focus almost exclusively on experiences for which there is evidence of clinical death.

2. **Are there any biblical examples of near-death experiences?**

   I believe so. Consider this account of what happened to the apostle Paul: "They stoned Paul and dragged him outside the city, thinking he was dead. But after the disciples had gathered around him, he got up and went back into the city" (Acts 14:19-20, NIV). If a man is stoned to death and considered dead but gets back up and tells of an encounter with the God of heaven, that's an NDE. And this may be what Paul later described when he said of himself, "I know a man in Christ who fourteen years ago was caught up to the third heaven" (2 Corinthians 12:2, NIV). Others who may have had an NDE include Lazarus (John 11:1-44), the twelve-year-old girl Jesus raised to life (Mark 5:35-43), the young man Paul raised to life (Acts 20:7-12), and the widow's son Elijah raised to life (1 Kings 17:17-24). We just don't have the stories of what they experienced while they were clinically dead. What we do know is that the Scriptures include testimonies of several people (such as Isaiah, Daniel, Ezekiel, Paul, and John) who had visions of heaven or were taken to heaven and saw God, and what they reported correlates with what NDErs commonly report today.

3. **Why should we trust people who claim to have had a near-death experience?**

While I do think NDE stories are evidence from God of his existence and the reality of heaven and hell, I do not advocate putting our trust in NDE stories. I want people to trust in God based on what he's revealed of himself in Scripture—and in *Imagine the God of Heaven*, I show how you can know that God inspired the prophets to write the Scriptures. I think it's better to see NDE stories as testimonies of God's existence and the reality of the afterlife, just as we would the testimony of someone who had a personal experience of God in their everyday life. We are wise to evaluate human testimonies based on how they align with God's self-revelation in Scripture. It's no different than what happened among people who saw Jesus heal people and raise the dead. Some concluded he was the Messiah, but others said his power to perform miracles came from Satan (John 8:48). NDErs interpret their experiences in light of their background and biases, as any of us would. That's why I'm not asking you to trust NDErs but rather to see how what they commonly report (as opposed to how they interpret it) aligns with God's revelation in Scripture.

4. **The Bible says, "People are destined to die once, and after that to face judgment" (Hebrews 9:27, NIV). How should this inform our understanding of near-death experiences?**

   It's important to understand that a near-death experience is not full biological death or entrance into eternal life. A commonality of NDE stories is encountering a border or boundary that NDErs say they knew they could not cross and still come back to earth. In some cases, Jesus tells the person, "You have not died yet; you must go back." An NDE is not the same as crossing over into eternity—it's an experience somewhere between life on earth and the life to come. So when the Bible says, "People are destined to die once, and after that to face judgment," this refers to permanent death and eternal life. What NDErs experience does not contradict Hebrews 9:27 because they do not cross the boundary into eternal life but come back to earth. Further, the judgments spoken of in the Bible—the great white throne judgment (Revelation 20:11-15) and the so-called *bema* seat judgment pertaining to rewards for deeds done on earth (2 Corinthians 5:10)—don't happen until the conclusion of human history. So when NDErs experience a sort of life review in their NDE, this is not the same thing as God's judgment. Rather, it seems to be more a validation of Jesus' words that everything that is secret will be made known, even our secret thoughts and motives (Luke 8:17; 1 Corinthians 4:5).

5. **What about the Scripture passages that say no one has seen God? Shouldn't we reject these claims of NDErs who say they've seen God?**

   Probably the most seemingly problematic statement relative to NDEs is Jesus' assertion that "no one has seen the Father except the one who is from God; only he has seen the Father" (John 6:46, NIV). A key principle of interpretation is to always interpret Scripture in light of Scripture. So, what must Jesus mean by saying, "No one has seen the Father," when Isaiah, Ezekiel, and Daniel all claimed to have seen God on his throne (Isaiah 6; Ezekiel 1; Daniel 7; Revelation 4)? Clearly, what NDErs claim to see does not contradict Scripture if what the prophets say aligns with Jesus' words. As I discuss in *Imagine the God of Heaven*, I believe Jesus is referring to the transcendent greatness of the infinite, eternal God whose being exceeds even what people in heaven can see or comprehend. Even in heaven we are not infinite in nature, so we can't "see" all of God. In that sense, no one has fully seen God except Jesus, the Son, who is one with God.

6. **Jesus said, "No one has ever gone into heaven except the one who came from heaven—the Son of Man" (John 3:13, NIV). Doesn't this discredit those who claim to see heaven in their NDE?**

   On first take, this can be a confusing statement. Jesus would have been well acquainted with the Scriptures written by prophets such as Isaiah, Daniel, and Ezekiel who had seen heaven (which aligns with what NDErs see). In context, he's talking to Nicodemus, who also knew and studied the Prophets but was struggling to believe the mysteries of heaven Jesus was revealing. Likely, what Jesus is saying here is that either he is the only one who can come and go from heaven of his own accord, or he is making the point that he understands the ways of the heavenly Father in a uniquely intimate way because he is the one who descended from heaven. Regardless, NDEr reports align with something experienced later by John when God says to him, "Come up here," followed by John's report, "At once I was in the Spirit, and there before me was a throne in heaven with someone sitting on it" (Revelation 4:1-2, NIV).

7. **Is it possible that people who have had near-death experiences are being deceived by demons?**

   Evil is real, and it's deceptive—on earth and in the afterlife. I found it interesting that many Christian NDErs I interviewed told me they had a welcoming committee of people whom they knew were there to guide and *protect* them on their journey to heaven. I always ask, "Protect you from what?" They don't know, but they intuitively knew in their NDE that those who came to meet them were there to protect them from something. So it appears that NDErs need protection, possibly from demonic interference, and without that protection could possibly be deceived by the demonic. How do we discern whether an NDEr has been deceived? By checking what they say with Scripture. God has given much evidence that the prophets and Jesus spoke his words of truth. I've given ways we can know God spoke through the prophets in *Imagine the God of Heaven*. So, we should always evaluate what NDErs say against what Jesus and the prophets taught. In some cases, I believe it's also possible that NDErs can have a "truthful" experience, but later interpret that experience in ways that evil twists into partial truths, leading them and others away from following God.

8. **Can NDE stories be useful in pointing people toward God?**

   I believe that NDE stories are a gift from God to our globally connected world. They are testimonies from around the world of God's identity, love, forgiveness, and compassion that align with what the Bible teaches. I believe these stories provide a line of evidence for a new apologetic, capable of pointing people everywhere to the God who created us all for his love. These stories are well known and widely studied. What's missing is helping people see how they align with God's revelation, which is what I try to do in *Imagine the God of Heaven*.

9. **Aren't you in danger of adding to Scripture by giving credence to these extra-biblical reports, some of which seem pretty wild?**

   Not at all. I like to think of NDEs not as new revelations but as enhancing the picture the Bible has already given us with more vivid color and detail. In other words, they enhance the understanding of the information we already have. An analogy would be watching a beautiful sunset from the shores of Hawaii while meditating on the verse, "The whole earth is full of his glory" (Isaiah 6:3, NIV).

The beauty of the surroundings isn't providing new revelation but providing vivid clarity and color that enhance the biblical truth that the world is full of God's glory. If an NDEr says something that does not align with Scripture, reject it.

10. **How can you endorse the validity of NDE reports when some have gone on to occult practices or contacting the dead? Doesn't this prove all NDEs are deceptions meant to lead people away from the Bible and Jesus?**

    It is true that some who have an NDE come back and seek out occult-like practices. But others come back, seek God, and find faith in Jesus. This should not surprise us since those who watched Jesus do miracles during his earthly ministry also had differing responses—some believed in him, and some denounced him. Every good gift from God can be twisted by evil. For example, while sex is a good gift from God (read Song of Songs), people have caused much harm by misusing it. Does that mean sex is evil? No, it means we should help people see what God intended when he gave us the gift of sex. The same is true with NDEs. They are meant to be a gift to help us discover that God is who he says he is and that he loves us.

11. **How do you account for those who see God or Jesus in their NDE but are clearly not believers prior to dying?**

    It is not unbiblical for nonbelievers to see the risen Jesus. The apostle John wrote, "Every eye will see him, even those who pierced him" (Revelation 1:7, NIV). Paul was an unbeliever when he saw this same God of Light, who then identified himself as Jesus. And Paul was not converted just because he saw Jesus. In fact, Jesus did not share the gospel with Paul but only told Paul, "Go into the city, and you will be told what you must do" (Acts 9:6, NIV). Once there, it was a disciple named Ananias who told Paul what to do to be saved. Paul still had a choice. So it should not surprise us that unbelievers see the God of Light and Love and feel loved, yet God does not make the gospel clear in their NDE. God has always used people to tell other people about him, and he wants us to first make the choice to seek him; then we find him.

12. **Don't NDEs promote universalism, that we're all going to heaven regardless of belief?**

    Not at all. There are heavenly NDEs, and there are hellish NDEs. If anything, NDEs clarify the reality of all that Jesus taught. It's also important to realize that NDEs are not indications of someone's final destination. I may be invited to visit Buckingham Palace, but that does not mean I'm being adopted into the royal family to live there forever. NDEs are just visits, not permanent residence. So we can't draw conclusions about who goes to heaven or hell based on their NDE. I found in my research that some NDEs start off wonderful, and if they had ended there, the NDEr would have concluded, "Atheists go to heaven." But then the person realized they were being deceived and were led into an outer darkness similar to what Jesus warned about. That's why I'm trying to show how NDEs fit within the bigger picture of God's revelation.

13. Paul wrote, "Satan disguises himself as an angel of light" (2 Corinthians 11:14). How do we know the God of Light NDErs encounter is not a deceptive spirit?

I'm not sure if Paul was being literal or metaphorical here. The context in which he made the statement is discerning false teachers, so it could be Paul is referring to "light" in the sense that Satan can cloak his temptations to make them appear to be good. For example, when Satan tempted Eve, he appealed to her by saying that eating from the forbidden tree would make her wise like God, knowing good and evil. He pretends he's bringing us light, yet his temptations enslave us in darkness. But if Paul meant that Satan literally appears as an angel of light, I am certain Satan could not also disguise himself to the point of conveying God's attributes. Many NDErs say things like, "This God of Light is the pinnacle of all love in whose presence I've never felt such overwhelming love." Love comes from God, and Satan rejected God's love and leadership and was cast out of heaven. Jesus says Satan is a murderer and a liar, and Jesus implies that evil is incapable of love (see John 8:42-44). So it's hard to imagine that the God of Light and Love NDErs encounter is Satan disguised as God. However, it's also true that someone can encounter the true God of Light and Love in an NDE yet still be deceived into a false understanding of what their NDE means. Again, that's why it's so important to first understand the bigger picture of God's revelation throughout history so we can wisely discern NDE stories.

Acknowledgments

We so appreciate the team of people responsible for helping to make this devotional a reality. We are deeply grateful for our agent, Don Gates, whose motivating guidance and care as a ministry partner has been invaluable. And Jack Kuhatschek, who made the time to assist us in organizing the story excerpts—what a huge help. We are so blessed to get to work with Jon Farrar, who shepherded the manuscript through to completion. Carol Travor and Erin Gwynne were so thorough, and we appreciate their excellence in editing the book. Thanks also to Elizabeth Czajkowski, Dean Renninger, and Stephanie Rische and her team for all their thoughtful, careful work in making this devotional as excellent and as beautiful as it can be. We want to give a special thank you to our friend Tom Jeannett, who prayed for us and cheered us on even before we started writing it up until we finished, and Kathy's mother, Mary Lou, for her continual, prayerful support. And of course, we are deeply grateful to all our friends in this book who shared their stories to radiate God's love to the world.

Notes

1. “Sarah W Probable NDE,” Near-Death Experience Research Foundation (NDERF), accessed January 17, 2023, https://www.nderf.org/Experiences/1sarah_w_probable_nde.html. NDERF excerpts used with permission of Jeffrey Long and Jody Long, founders and administrators of the Near-Death Experience Research Foundation.
2. Erica McKenzie, *Dying to Fit In* (self-pub., CreateSpace, 2015), loc. 68, Kindle. Used with permission.
3. Dr. Ron Smothermon, “My Near-Death Experience During a Murder Attempt” (unpublished manuscript), Microsoft Word file. Used with permission.
4. Randy Kay, personal interview with John Burke, Austin, Texas, April 18, 2023. Used with permission.
5. Jim Woodford, personal interview with John Burke, Austin, Texas, April 18, 2023. Used with permission.
6. Jim Woodford with Dr. Thom Gardner, *Heaven, an Unexpected Journey: One Man's Experience with Heaven, Angels, and the Afterlife* (Shippensburg, PA: Destiny Image, 2017), 110.
7. Dean Braxton, phone interview with John Burke, August 10, 2022. Used with permission.
8. Kevin Zadai, “What Jesus Warned Me about in Heaven Will Shock You,” Supernatural Stories, October 8, 2020, YouTube video, https://www.youtube.com/watch?v=CyYHlYPEpfQ&list=PLWqRBgNjtFbdrqLTICgh_6gHJDJUs589j&index=2&t=2s. Used with permission.
9. Zadai, “What Jesus Warned Me about in Heaven Will Shock You.”
10. Dr. Colin Perry, Zoom interview with John Burke, October 5, 2022. Used with permission. For more, see C. Thomas Perry, *Dying to Be Alive* (self-pub., Xlibris, 2015).
11. Mark McDonough, “House Fire Kills Family and Burns Most of Surgeon's Body as Teen. Next, He Meets Them in Heaven,” interview by Randy Kay, Randy Kay Ministries, September 3, 2022, YouTube video, https://www.youtube.com/watch?v=DVdkjJA-Ycc. Used with permission of Mark McDonough. Includes minor edits by Dr. Mark McDonough.

12. Mark D. McDonough, *Forged through Fire: A Reconstructive Surgeon's Story of Survival, Faith, and Healing* (Grand Rapids, MI: Revell, 2019), 75.
13. McDonough, "House Fire Kills Family," video interview by Randy Kay. Includes minor edits by Dr. Mark McDonough.
14. McDonough, *Forged through Fire*; McDonough, "House Fire Kills Family," video interview by Randy Kay. Includes minor edits by Dr. Mark McDonough.
15. Diana Shepherd, Zoom interview with John Burke, February 24, 2022. Used with permission.
16. Dr. Ron Smothermon, phone interview with John Burke, May 13, 2022. Used with permission. Some quotes also taken from Smothermon, "My Near-Death Experience During a Murder Attempt."
17. Smothermon, phone interview with John Burke, May 13, 2022; Smothermon, "My Near-Death Experience During a Murder Attempt."
18. Jim Woodford, personal interview with Kathy Burke, April 18, 2023. Used with permission.
19. Woodford, personal interview with John Burke, April 18, 2023.
20. Woodford, personal interview with Kathy Burke, April 18, 2023.
21. Woodford, personal interview with John Burke, April 18, 2023.
22. Woodford, personal interview with Kathy Burke, April 18, 2023.
23. Woodford, personal interview with John Burke, April 18, 2023.
24. Woodford, personal interview with Kathy Burke, April 18, 2023.
25. Heidi Barr, personal interview with John Burke, April 7, 2020. Used with permission. Some quotes also taken from Heidi Barr, "Your Life Is in Good Hands" (unpublished manuscript), PDF. Used with permission.
26. Penny Wittbrodt, Zoom interview with John Burke, September 28, 2022. Used with permission.
27. Cedric [Swidiq] Kanana with Benjamin Fischer, *I Once Was Dead: How God Rescued Me from Islam, Drugs, Witchcraft, and Even Death* (Oasis International, 2022), loc. 84–116, Kindle. Used with permission of Oasis International and Cedric Kanana.
28. Dean Braxton, personal interview with John Burke, April 18, 2023. Used with permission.
29. Dean Braxton, personal interview with John Burke, Austin, Texas, September 26, 2019. Used with permission.
30. Braxton, personal interview with John Burke, April 18, 2023.
31. Braxton, personal interview with John Burke, September 26, 2019.
32. Dean Braxton, "Experiencing the Throne of God," in Sid Roth and Lonnie Lane, *Heaven Is Beyond Your Wildest Expectations: Ten True Stories of Experiencing Heaven* (Destiny Image), loc. 1–3, Kindle.
33. Woodford, personal interview with John Burke, April 18, 2023.

34. D. S. Weiler, *Dead Is Just a Four Letter Word* (self-published, 2007), http://www.1way2see.com/thebook.html.
35. Randy Kay, *Heaven Stormed* (Destiny Image, 2024), 79–80, endorser copy.
36. Zadai, "What Jesus Warned Me about in Heaven Will Shock You."
37. McDonough, *Forged through Fire*, 75.
38. Cheri Henderson, "Dr. Mark McDonough: Burn Victim Turned Plastic Surgeon," *Orlando*, August 7, 2020, https://www.orlandomagazine.com/dr-mark-mcdonough-burn-victim-turned-plastic-surgeon.
39. Perry, Zoom interview with John Burke, October 5, 2022.
40. "Catherine NDE," Near-Death Experience Research Foundation (NDERF), https://www.nderf.org/Experiences/1catherine_nde_8697.html.
41. McKenzie, *Dying to Fit In*, loc. 73–74.
42. Greggory Rickert, phone interview with John Burke, July 20, 2022. Used with permission.
43. Dr. Ron Smothermon, personal interview with Kathy Burke, Austin, Texas, April 18, 2023. Used with permission.
44. Braxton, personal interview with John Burke, April 18, 2023.
45. William Smith, "In Realms of Glory," in Roth and Lane, *Heaven Is Beyond Your Wildest Expectations*, loc. 136–137.
46. Smothermon, "My Near-Death Experience during a Murder Attempt."
47. Howard Storm, *My Descent into Death: A Second Chance at Life* (Potter/TenSpeed/Harmony), loc. 382–388, Kindle.
48. Kay, *Heaven Stormed*, 79–80.
49. Marvin J. Besteman and Lorilee Craker, *My Journey to Heaven: What I Saw and How It Changed My Life* (Baker Publishing Group, 2012), loc. 75–76, Kindle.
50. Rebecca Ruter Springer, *Intra Muros* (Elgin, IL: David C. Cook Publishing, 1898), 156–158.
51. "Micki P NDE," Near-Death Experience Research Foundation (NDERF), accessed January 18, 2023, https://www.nderf.org/Experiences/1micki_p_nde.html.
52. "Jeff S NDE," Near-Death Experience Research Foundation (NDERF), accessed January 22, 2023, https://www.nderf.org/Experiences/1jeff_s_nde.html.
53. Father Cedric Pisegna, phone interview with John Burke, September 15, 2022. Used with permission.
54. Father Cedric Pisegna, *Death: The Final Surrender* (Houston, TX: Passionist Publications, 2013, 2022), 87. Used with permission. Includes minor edits and additions by Father Cedric Pisegna.

55. Wayne Fowler, Zoom interview with John Burke, November 1, 2021. Used with permission.
56. Steve Kang, Zoom interview with John Burke, November 9, 2022. Used with permission.
57. Ian McCormack, quoted in Jenny Sharkey, *Clinically Dead: I've Seen Heaven and Hell* (self-pub., CreateSpace, 2012, 2013), loc. 16, Kindle.
58. Ivan Tuttle, personal interview with John Burke, Greenville, South Carolina, March 18, 2022. Used with permission.
59. Gary L. Wood, *A Place Called Heaven* (Kingwood, TX: RevMedia Publishing, 2013), loc. 322–332, Kindle.
60. McKenzie, *Dying to Fit In*, loc. 68, Kindle.
61. McKenzie, *Dying to Fit In*, loc. 74, 76, 79, Kindle.
62. "Julie H Probable NDE," Near-Death Experience Research Foundation (NDERF), accessed January 22, 2023, https://www.nderf.org/Experiences/1julie_h_probable_nde.html.
63. Jeremy, email message to John Burke, February 10, 2021. Used with permission. The Scripture referenced in this quotation is a paraphrase of Matthew 12:50.
64. Susanne Seymoure, Zoom interview with John Burke, February 28, 2022. Used with permission.
65. Pisegna, phone interview with John Burke, September 15, 2022; Pisegna, *Death: The Final Surrender*, loc. 65–66, Kindle.
66. Braxton, personal interview with John Burke, April 18, 2023.
67. Rajiv Parti with Paul Perry, *Dying to Wake Up: A Doctor's Voyage into the Afterlife and the Wisdom He Brought Back* (New York: Atria Books, 2016), 30.
68. Dr. Rajiv Parti, "OBE: Dr. Rajiv Parti," All Reality Video, November 19, 2013, YouTube video, https://www.youtube.com/watch?v=2EFAq_aQkJc.
69. Parti, *Dying to Wake Up*, 32–34; "Dying to Wake Up: A True NDE Story with Dr. Rajiv Parti," interview by Curry Stegen, Passion for the Paranormal, September 18, 2019, YouTube audio, https://www.youtube.com/watch?v=inHo47fYYYA&t=1076s.
70. Parti, *Dying to Wake Up*, 42.
71. Rajiv Parti, "My Epiphany: Christ Consciousness and Universal Love," Raj Parti, MD, accessed January 19, 2023, https://rajpartimd.com/my-epiphany/.
72. Howard Storm, personal interview with John Burke, Austin, Texas, February 25, 2016. Used with permission.
73. Barr, "Your Life Is in Good Hands."
74. Barr, "Your Life Is in Good Hands."
75. Barr, "Your Life Is in Good Hands."
76. Braxton, phone interview with John Burke, August 10, 2022.

77. Richard Sigmund, "A Picture of Life in Heaven" in Sid Roth and Lonnie Lane, *Heaven Is Beyond Your Wildest Expectations: Ten True Stories of Experiencing Heaven* (Shippensburg, PA: Destiny Image, 2012), loc. 118–119, Kindle.
78. Kay, personal interview with John Burke, April 18, 2023.
79. Ian McCormack, quoted in Jenny Sharkey, *Clinically Dead: I've Seen Heaven and Hell* (Gospel Media, 2013), 588, 600–626.
80. Wittbrodt, Zoom interview with John Burke, September 28, 2022.
81. Wittbrodt, Zoom interview with John Burke, September 28, 2022.
82. Seymoure, Zoom interview with John Burke, February 28, 2022.
83. Susanne Seymoure, *My Secrets from Heaven: A Child's Trip to Heaven and Back* (White Birch, LLC, 2017), 56. Used with permission.
84. Seymoure, *My Secrets from Heaven*, 70.
85. Seymoure, *My Secrets from Heaven*, 56.
86. Susanne Seymoure, phone interview with John Burke, August 5, 2022. Used with permission.
87. Woodford, personal interview with John Burke, April 18, 2023.
88. Jim Woodford, phone interview with John Burke, December 9, 2022. Used with permission.
89. Kay, personal interview with John Burke, April 18, 2023.
90. Kay, personal interview with John Burke, April 18, 2023.
91. "Mary NDE," Near-Death Experience Research Foundation (NDERF), accessed January 14, 2023, https://www.nderf.org/Experiences/1mary_nde.html.
92. "Mary NDE," Near-Death Experience Research Foundation (NDERF).
93. Captain Dale Black, personal interview with John Burke, Austin, Texas, September 26, 2019. Used with permission.
94. Dale Black with Ken Gire, *Flight to Heaven: A Plane Crash . . . A Lone Survivor . . . A Journey to Heaven—and Back* (Grand Rapids, MI: Baker Publishing Group, 2010), loc. 99–100, Kindle.
95. See Matthew 17:1-5 (Jesus' transfiguration) and Exodus 24:16 (God's appearance on Mount Sinai). Both refer to a cloud accompanying God.
96. Braxton, phone interview with John Burke, August 10, 2022.
97. Rickert, phone interview with John Burke, July 20, 2022.
98. Pisegna, phone interview with John Burke, September 15, 2022.
99. Pisegna, *Death: The Final Surrender*, 102–103, 114, 93. Includes minor edits and additions by Father Cedric Pisegna.
100. "Alexa H NDE," Near-Death Experience Research Foundation (NDERF), accessed January 20, 2023, https://www.nderf.org/Experiences/1alexa_h_nde.html. Includes minor edits and additions by Alexa Hartung sent to Kathy Burke via email, January 5, 2023.

101. Bibi Tahereh and Saeed Edina Abedini, personal interview with John Burke, Austin, Texas, April 19, 2019; Tahereh and Edina, phone interview with John Burke, March 7, 2022. Used with permission.
102. Tahereh and Edina, personal interview with John Burke, April 19, 2019; Tahereh and Edina, phone interview with John Burke, March 7, 2022.
103. Tahereh and Edina, personal interview with John Burke, April 19, 2019; Tahereh and Edina, phone interview with John Burke, March 7, 2022.
104. Tahereh and Edina, personal interview with John Burke, April 19, 2019.
105. Wittbrodt, Zoom interview with John Burke, September 28, 2022.
106. *Merriam-Webster*, s.v. "fix" verb, http://www.merriam-webster.com/dictionary/fix.
107. Springer, *Intra Muros*, 11–12.
108. Springer, *Intra Muros*, 60–61.
109. Springer, *Intra Muros*, 64–65.
110. Springer, *Intra Muros*, 120.
111. Springer, *Intra Muros*, 91.
112. C. S. Lewis, *Letters to Malcolm: Chiefly on Prayer* (New York: Harcourt, Brace and World, 1963; New York: HarperCollins, 2017), ch. 17.
113. Smothermon, "My Near-Death Experience During a Murder Attempt."
114. Perry, Zoom interview with John Burke, October 5, 2022. For more, see Perry, *Dying to Be Alive*.
115. "Micki P NDE," Near-Death Experience Research Foundation (NDERF), accessed January 22, 2023, https://www.nderf.org/Experiences/1micki_p_nde.html.
116. Jeremy, email message to John Burke, February 10, 2021.
117. "Julie H Probable NDE," Near-Death Experience Research Foundation (NDERF).
118. Braxton, personal interview with John Burke, April 18, 2023.
119. Braxton, personal interview with John Burke, April 18, 2023.
120. Wittbrodt, Zoom interview with John Burke, September 28, 2022.
121. Kay, *Heaven Stormed*, 117–118.
122. Richard Eby, "Experiencing Heaven, Experiencing Hell," in Sid Roth and Lonnie Lane, *Heaven Is Beyond Your Wildest Expectations: Ten True Stories of Experiencing Heaven* (Shippensburg, PA: Destiny Image, 2012), loc. 1669, Kindle.
123. Gary L. Wood, *I Saw the Glories of Heaven: A Story of Healing, Hope, and Life after Death* (New Kensington, PA: Whitaker House, 2008, 2014, 2018), loc. 455–470, Kindle.
124. Santosh Acharjee, phone interview with John Burke, November 15, 2022. Used with permission.

125. Santosh (Sandy) Acharjee, *My Encounter with Jesus at Heaven's Gates: A Life-Changing Near-Death Experience* (Bloomington, IN: AuthorHouse, 2016), loc. 600–650, Kindle. The last sentence in this paragraph is taken from Acharjee, phone interview with John Burke, November 15, 2022.
126. Parti, "My Epiphany."
127. Braxton, personal interview with John Burke, April 18, 2023.
128. Black, personal interview with John Burke, September 26, 2019.
129. Pisegna, *Death: The Final Surrender*, 82.
130. Pisegna, phone interview with John Burke, September 15, 2022.
131. Pisegna, phone interview with John Burke, September 15, 2022.
132. Woodford, personal interview with Kathy Burke, April 18, 2023.
133. Kay, *Heaven Stormed*, 135–136.
134. Zadai, "What Jesus Warned Me about in Heaven Will Shock You."
135. Zadai, "What Jesus Warned Me about in Heaven Will Shock You."
136. Braxton, phone interview with John Burke, August 10, 2022.
137. Braxton, personal interview with John Burke, April 18, 2023.
138. Kay, personal interview with John Burke, April 18, 2023.
139. Heidi Barr, phone interview with John Burke, September 20, 2022. Used with permission.
140. "Sarah W Probable NDE," Near-Death Experience Research Foundation (NDERF).
141. Acharjee, phone interview with John Burke, November 15, 2022.
142. Acharjee, *My Encounter with Jesus at Heaven's Gates*, loc. 28, Kindle.
143. Acharjee, *My Encounter with Jesus at Heaven's Gates*, loc. 600–650, Kindle.
144. Santosh Acharjee, personal interview with John Burke, April 18, 2023. Used with permission.
145. Springer, *Intra Muros*, 30–31.
146. Braxton, personal interview with John Burke, April 18, 2023.
147. Karina Martinez, Zoom interview with John Burke, April 28, 2022. Used with permission.
148. Woodford, personal interview with Kathy Burke, April 18, 2023.
149. Kay, *Heaven Stormed*, 102–103.
150. Rickert, phone interview with John Burke, July 20, 2022.
151. Rickert, phone interview with John Burke, July 20, 2022.
152. "Alexa H NDE," Near-Death Experience Research Foundation (NDERF). Includes minor edits and additions by Alexa Hartung.
153. Braxton, phone interview with John Burke, August 10, 2022.
154. Barr, "Your Life Is in Good Hands."
155. Smothermon, "My Near-Death Experience During a Murder Attempt."

156. Dr. Ron Smothermon, personal interview with John Burke, Austin, Texas, April 18, 2023. Used with permission.
157. Smothermon, "My Near-Death Experience During a Murder Attempt."
158. Braxton, phone interview with John Burke, August 10, 2022.
159. Seymoure, Zoom interview with John Burke, February 28, 2022.
160. Erica McKenzie, personal interview with John Burke, Austin, Texas, April 18, 2023. Used with permission.
161. Kay, *Heaven Stormed*, 107–108.
162. Howard Storm, personal interview with John Burke, Austin, Texas, October 26, 2015. Used with permission.
163. Tony Davis, paraphrased from interview with Randy Kay, "Shot Multiple Times by Gang Member – Died and Was Lead to Heaven by Angels," posted October 28, 2022, by Randy Kay, YouTube, https://www.youtube.com/watch?v=_FxxyTE80WE.
164. "Douglas D NDE," Near-Death Experience Research Foundation (NDERF), accessed January 27, 2023, https://www.nderf.org/Experiences/1douglas_d_nde_3107.html.
165. See Acts 22:6-16.
166. Braxton, "Experiencing the Throne of God," in Roth and Lane, *Heaven Is Beyond Your Wildest Expectations*, loc. 2–3, Kindle.
167. Pisegna, *Death: The Final Surrender*, loc. 78–79, Kindle.
168. Santosh Acharjee, "Near-Death Experience: Hindu Man Dies and Faces Gate to Heaven and Hell," video interview by Randy Kay, Randy Kay Ministries, April 24, 2022, https://www.youtube.com/watch?v=Utcf052XGx8.
169. Acharjee, phone interview with John Burke, November 15, 2022; Acharjee, *My Encounter with Jesus at Heaven's Gates*, loc. 1259–1274, Kindle.
170. "Sarah W Probable NDE," Near-Death Experience Research Foundation (NDERF).
171. Jim Woodford, Zoom video call interview with John Burke, November 23, 2022. Used with permission.
172. Woodford, personal interview with Kathy Burke, April 18, 2023.
173. Braxton, personal interview with John Burke, September 26, 2019.
174. Sigmund, "A Picture of Life in Heaven," in Roth and Lane, *Heaven Is Beyond Your Wildest Expectations*, loc. 120, Kindle.
175. McKenzie, *Dying to Fit In*, loc. 74, 76, 79, Kindle.
176. Wittbrodt, Zoom interview with John Burke, September 28, 2022.
177. "Alexa H NDE," Near-Death Experience Research Foundation (NDERF). Includes minor edits and additions by Alexa Hartung.
178. Dr. Mary Neal, personal interview with John Burke, Austin, Texas, February 22, 2016. Used with permission.

About the Authors

John Burke is the author of the *New York Times* bestsellers *Imagine Heaven* and *Imagine the God of Heaven*, along with *No Perfect People Allowed, Soul Revolution*, and *Unshockable Love*. He and his wife, Kathy, founded Gateway Community Church, a multisite church based in Austin, Texas, and recently Imagine Heaven Ministries. As an international speaker and leading expert on how NDEs correlate with the Bible, John has addressed hundreds of thousands of people in thirty countries on topics of leadership, spiritual growth, and the exhilarating life to come. He recently launched the *Imagine Heaven Podcast with John Burke* on YouTube and all podcast platforms.

Kathy Burke cofounded Gateway Community Church in Austin and is a freelance writer and editor. She is the primary author of the *Imagine Heaven Devotional* and contributed to *Imagine Heaven* and *Imagine the God of Heaven*. Kathy has worked in ministry for over three decades, along with twenty years as a home educator, and is now writing books, including a forthcoming children's book on heaven. The Burkes have two married children and two grandchildren.

Keep in touch with John and Kathy through their website: ImagineHeaven.net.

TO CONNECT WITH

JOHN **BURKE**

SEARCH ONLINE FOR
"AUTHOR JOHN BURKE"

SPEAKING EVENTS

BOOKS

CONTACT

OTHER FREE RESOURCES

CP1903